David Gascoyne was born in 1916 and educated at Salisbury Cathedral Choir School and Regent Street Polytechnic. His first book of poems, *Roman Balcony*, was published in 1932, and the following year his only novel, *Opening Day*, appeared. *A Short Survey of Surrealism* (1935) was followed by his second book of poems, *Man's Life Is This Meat* (1936). In 1938 he published *Hölderlin's Madness*, a collection of translations of the German poet, with verse commentary. He was one of the four poets in *Poets of Tomorrow 3* (1942). His other poetical works are *Poems 1937–42* (published 1943), *The Vagrant and Other Poems* (1950) and *Night Thoughts* (1956). His *Collected Poems* came out in 1965. He is renowned as a translator of contemporary French poetry and a volume of his collected translations is currently in preparation.

W. S. Graham was born at Greenock, Scotland, in 1918 and has published several books of verse: *Cage Without Grievance*, *The Seven Journeys*, *2nd Poems*, *The White Threshold*, *The Nightfishing* and *Malcolm Mooney's Land*. He has read his own verse on radio and television, held readings in the U.S.A., and given a series of lectures at New York University. Recently some of his new poems have appeared in periodicals in America and this country.

Kathleen Raine, born in 1908, was educated at Girton College, Cambridge, where she took a degree in natural sciences, and later returned for some years as a research fellow. Among her more recent publications have been a book of poems, *The Hollow Hill* (1965), *Defending Ancient Springs* (criticism, 1967), *William Blake and Traditional Mythology* (1968), the Andrew Mellon Lectures at the National Gallery of Art, Washington D.C. for 1962, and *Thomas Taylor* (selected writings) in collaboration with George Mills Harper (1969). More recently she has given papers at the W. B. Yeats Summer School in Sligo, and at the (Jungian) *Eranos* conference at Ascra.

Penguin Modern Poets

17

DAVID GASCOYNE
W. S. GRAHAM
KATHLEEN RAINE

Penguin Books

Penguin Books Ltd, Harmondsworth, Middlesex, England
Penguin Books Inc., 7110 Ambassador Road, Baltimore, Maryland 21207, U.S.A.
Penguin Books Australia Ltd, Ringwood, Victoria, Australia

—

This selection first published 1970

—

Copyright © Penguin Books Ltd, 1970

—

Made and printed in Great Britain by
Cox & Wyman Ltd,
London, Reading and Fakenham
Set in Monotype Garamond

Contents

CONTENTS

Acknowledgements

For permission to reprint the poems in these selections grateful acknowledgement is made to the following publishers: for the poems by David Gascoyne, selected from *Collected Poems*, 1965, to Oxford University Press in association with André Deutsch; for 'Part of a Poem in Progress', first published in the *Malahat Review*, Victoria, British Columbia, to the author; for the poems by W. S. Graham, from *The White Threshold*, 1949, *The Nightfishing*, 1955, *Malcolm Mooney's Land*, 1970, to Faber & Faber; for the poems by Kathleen Raine, from *Collected Poems*, 1956, and *The Hollow Hill*, 1965, to Hamish Hamilton.

DAVID GASCOYNE

[ONE]

1932–1936

The cold renunciatory beauty

The cold renunciatory beauty of those who would die
to hide their love from scornful fingers of the drab
is not that which glistens like wing or leaf in eyes
of erotic statues standing breast to chest
on high and open mountainside.

Complex draws tighter like a steel wire mesh
about the awkward bodies of those born under shame,
striping the tender flesh with blood like tears
flowing; their love they dare not name;
Each is divided by desire and fear.

The young songs of the hopeless blind shall strike
matches in the marble corridor and find
their bodies cool and white as the stone walls,
and shall embrace, emerging like mingled springs
onto the height to face the fearless sun.

The Unattained

On the evening of a day on the threshold of Summer,
Before the full blast of vertiginous Summer, I flung
This foursquare body down upon the crumpled ground,
Moist with a dew-like sweat; and on all sides heard
The ceaseless clicking and fret of insect swarms;
I felt energy drain from these limbs spread cruciform,
Dribble away like sap from crushed bracken's veins;
Felt this my heaviness upon acid-green grass and sand,
Under the passive sky, becoming magnetic as stone;
And my lids slid down over eyes fanned by coloured winds.

And fierce desires swelled up from out my quiet:
To pierce through this flesh outwards, to embrace
The eternal blue, against my nostrils to smother
The fragrant cotton of the clouds; to feel beneath
Impatient soles of feet the grinding grit
Of gravel, the sharp sides of stones; and without end
Against the eyeballs' skin to press fresh images,
To lave in the swift stream of forms these avid eyes:
By passion suspended, hands stretched out, gnawed
From within, O how and to where could I pass?

Not within facile grasp swings that unattainable globe:
Tho' to catch an echo of the spheres' music these ears strain,
And nostrils yearn for the rich scent of flame and of blood,
Hands strive clumsily phantom's ambiguous flesh to caress,
In vain the inward divinity batters against the gates,
Kicking against the pricks until the urgent spirit breaks.
Hourly the ocean, World's clock, smashes against the cliffs;
And savage relentless Time shreds onwards through the
  skull,

Whispers: 'Come home, only Death burns out there.'
  And I know
That this is my body, my cell, and I am alone and prone.

After a plenitude of defeat, a load of sorrow.
Forget your coward victories, your crown of thorns,
And send the sulky eye-witness away;
Block out that solitary figure, the proud
Indomitable one. Hack down the heavy black
Statue. And because you can only remember
The darkest days of defeat, your weariness,
Because you can see but death's sinister finger
Always pointing to the shadowed wall,
Raise no more gloomy monuments, or build
A more transparent wall.
                                    And listen
To the rich voice like flute-voice breaking
Suddenly from the white marble larynx;
Sunlight breaking suddenly upon the naked torso
Like the rustling down of a flimsy dress.
Listening, join proud singing with the voice,
As the sound of an inland sea now freed,
Smashing its winter cage of ice and rushing
With liquid arms and hands of foam uplifted
Across the frozen lands toward the outer seas.

No Solution

Above and below
The roll of days spread out like a cloth
Days engraved on everyone's forehead
Yesterday folding To-morrow opening
To-day like a horse without a rider
To-day a drop of water falling into a lake
To-day a white light above and below

A fan of days held in a virgin hand
A burning taper burning paper
And you can turn back no longer
No longer stand still
The words of poems curling among the ashes
Hieroglyphics of larger despairs than ours.

The Last Head

In the warm sand-coloured room at the end of the watery
    road
I saw the last head with its fingers plaited in curls
And its sides ridged and smooth, worn by runnels of light.
The obvious table supported a map of the moon.

The faces in trees must be stopped, and the towers
And peninsular madness and gems
The canals are all stopped with a white-flowering weed
The beetle conspires to bring doom to the bridge
The night air is salt on the tongue. The white shields
In the stable fall clattering down from the walls.

But the last head is safe in its vegetable dome:
The last head is wrapped in its oiled silk sheath,
While the pale tepid flame of its ichorous brain
Consumes all its body's dry shells.

Purified Disgust

An impure sky
A heartless and impure breathing
The fevered breath of logic
And a great bird broke loose
Flapping into the silence with strident cries
A great bird with cruel claws

Beyond that savage pretence of knowledge
Beyond that posture of oblivious dream
Into the divided terrain of anguish
Where one walks with bound hands
Where one walks with knotted hair
With eyes searching the zenith
Where one walks like Sebastian

Heavy flesh invokes the voice of penitence
Seated at the stone tables
Seated at a banquet of the carnal lusts
Behind our putrid masks we snicker
Our men's heads behind our masks
Twisted from innocence to insolence

And there the pointing finger says and there
The pointing finger demonstrates
The accuser struggles with his accusation
The accused writhes and blusters
The finger points to the chosen victim
The victim embraces his victimization
The accused belches defiance

How could we touch that carrion?
A sudden spasm saves us
A pure disgust illumines us
The music of the spheres is silent
Our hands lie still upon the counterpane
And the herds come home.

Charity Week

TO MAX ERNST

Have presented the lion with medals of mud
One for each day of the week
One for each beast in this sombre menagerie
Shipwrecked among the clouds
Shattered by the violently closed eyelids

Garments of the seminary
Worn by the nocturnal expedition
By all the chimæras
Climbing in at the window
With lice in their hair
Noughts in their crosses
Ice in their eyes

Hysteria upon the staircase
Hair torn out by the roots
Lace handkerchiefs torn to shreds
And stained by tears of blood
Their fragments strewn upon the waters

These are the phenomena of zero
Invisible men on the pavement
Spittle in the yellow grass
The distant roar of disaster
And the great bursting womb of desire.

Unspoken

Words spoken leave no time for regret
Yet regret
The unviolated silence and
White sanctuses of sleep
Under the heaped veils
The inexorably prolonged vigils
Speech flowing away like water
With its undertow of violence and darkness
Carrying with it forever
All those formless vessels
Abandoned palaces
Tottering under the strain of being
Full-blossoming hysterias
Lavishly scattering their stained veined petals

In sleep there are places places
Places overlap
Yellow sleep in the afternoon sunlight
Coming invisibly in through the pinewood door
White sleep wrapped warm in the midwinter
Inhaling the tepid snow
And sleeping in April at night in sleeping in
Shadow as shallow as water and articulate with pain

Recurrent words
Slipping between the cracks
With the face of memory and the sound of its voice
More intimate than sweat at the roots of the hair
Frozen stiff in a moment and then melted
Swifter than air between the lips
Swifter to vanish than enormous buildings
Seen for a moment from the corners of the eyes

Travelling through man's enormous continent
No two roads the same
Nor ever the same names to places
Migrating towns and fluid boundaries
There are no settlers here there are
No solid stones

Travelling through man's unspoken continent
Among the unspeaking mountains
The dumb lakes and the deafened valleys
Illumined by paroxysms of vision
Clear waves of soundless sight
Lapping out of the heart of darkness
Flowing endless over buried speech
Drowning the words and words

And here I am caught up among the glistenings of
Bodies proud with the opulence of flesh
The silent limbs of beings lying across the light
Silken at the hips and pinched between two fingers
Their thirsty faces turned upwards towards breaking
Their long legs shifting slanting turning
In a parade of unknown virtues
Beginning again and beginning
Again

Till unspoken is unseen
Until unknown
Descending from knowledge to knowledge
A dim world uttering a voiceless cry
Spinning helpless between sleep and waking
A blossom scattered by a motionless wind
A wheel of fortune turning in the fog

Predicting the lucid moment
Casting the bodiless body from its hub
Back into the cycle of return and change
Breathing the mottled petals
Out across the circling seas
And foaming oceans of disintegration
Where navigate our daylight vessels
Following certain routes to uncertain lands

Antennae

1

A river of perfumed silk
A final glimpse of content
The girls are alone on the highroad.

2

In the evening there is a cry of despair
Silence begins spawning its myriad
Shifting away from the restless neon auras
Disturbed by the menacing gestures of starvation
The unchanging programme of its manoeuvres
Its rasping grasping claws.

3

The sun bursts through its skin
The last smooth man emerges from the tunnel
And flags burst into song along the streets
The morning's garlands pull themselves to pieces
And fly away in flocks

The sea is a bubble in a cup of salt
The earth is a grain of sand in a nutshell
The earth is blue.

4

Truth, fickle monster, gazed in at the open window
Longing to eat of the fruit of the poisoned tree
Longing to eat from the plates on our lozenge-shaped
 table
Fearing the truth

And the peaceful star of the vigil fell from the sky
And spilt its amazing fluids across the mosaic floor.

5

The timeless sleepers tangled in the bed
In the midst of the sonorous island, alone

The tongue between the teeth
The river between the sands

Love in my hand like lace
Your hand enlaced with mine.

6

A delicate breath a whisp of smoke
Floating between our eyes
The rainbow-coloured barque of pleasure
Brushing the fluid foliage aside
Derision's flimsy feathers

Between our eyes
The shadow of a smile.

7

The full breasts of eternity awaiting tender hands.

8

Not wholly unprepared
Nor entirely unafraid
Vigilant
Watching the colours

Discovered by morning:
Dispensation of doubtful benefits.

9

At least alone at last
When gone the body's warmth
The incisiveness of glances
The unwinding crimson thread
The given flower

Forgotten mouths forget.

10

For now we are suspended above life
There are a great many questions to be answered
A great many debts to be paid

So evanescent that which binds us
That more is meant, regret is absent . . .
Our burning possession of each other
Held in both hands because it is all we have.

Lozanne

It was seven, it was nine o'clock, the doors were closing, the windows were screaming. You bent over the shadow that lay on the floor and saw its eyes dissolving. The band about your forehead began to turn. The band of fever.

The armchair turned into a palace, the carpet became a bank of withered flowers, *and then it was time to go*. Every semblance of that which had gone before became the means by which you ascended the great staircase. And took your place among the stars.

For it is significant, is it not, that the *blemish* about which you were so insistent was nothing less than that interminable voice which haunted you in your dreams, saying 'I love you' over and over again. And the panelling of the room where they asked you questions was made of exactly the same wood as the mallet which you had to hate.

The dusty and ashen residue of a passion that now raged elsewhere, but still raged, rose slowly upwards to the surface of the lake as your blood sank slowly through it. And the other returned to ice. Oh, I can see through your eyes now and I can see what flame it was that melted everything before it! (Though the obstinate sod refused to become softened by the rain of thaw). But you were spared passing through that black box where a masked man kisses his victim before her death. I ask the glass again: Who gave the victims right to refuse life to those who refuse to be victimized?

Those who damned shall be damned.

The Diabolical Principle

The red dew of autumn clings to winter's curtains
And when the curtain rises the landscape is as empty as a
    board
Empty except for a broken bottle and a torso broken like a
    bottle
And when the curtain falls the palace of cards will fall
The card-castle on the table will topple without a sound

An eye winks from the shadow of the gallows
A tumbled bed slides upwards from the shadow
A suicide with mittened hands stumbles out of the lake
And writes a poem on the tablets of a dead man's heart
The last man but one climbs the scaffold and fades into
    the mist

The marine sceptre is splintered like an anvil
Its spine crackles with electric nerves
While eagle pinions thunder through the darkness
While swords and breastplates clatter in the darkness
And the storm falls across the bed like a thrice-doomed
    tree.

*

    A basket of poisoned arrows
    Severing seawrack, ships' tracks
    Leadentipped darts of disaster
    A unicorn champs at the waves
    The waves are green branches singing
    The cry of a foal at daybreak
    A broken mouth at sunset
    A broken lamp among the clouds' draperies

A sound drops into the water and the water boils
The sound of disastrous waves
Waves flood the room when the door opens
A white horse stamps upon the liquid floor
The sunlight is tiring to our opened eyes
And the sand is dead
Feet in the sand make patterns
Patterns flow like rivers to the distant sky
Rippling shells like careful signatures
A tangled skein of blood

In fumigated emptiness revolves the mind
The light laughs like an unposted letter
Railways rush into the hills.

*

A worm slithers from the earth and the shell is broken
A giant mazed misery tears the veil to shreds
Stop it tormentor stop the angry planet before it breaks
   the sky

Having shattered the untapped barrel
Having given up hope for water
Having shaken the chosen words in a hat
History opened its head like a wallet
And folded itself inside.

The Rites of Hysteria

In the midst of the flickering sonorous islands
The islands with liquid gullets full of mistletoe-suffering
Where untold truths are hidden in fibrous baskets
And the cold mist of decayed psychologies stifles the sun
An arrow hastening through the zone of basaltic honey
An arrow choked by suppressed fidgetings and smokey
    spasms
An arrow with lips of cheese was caught by a floating hair

The perfumed lenses whose tongues were tied up with
    wire
The boxes of tears and the bicycles coated with stains
Swam out of their false-bottomed nests into clouds of
    dismay
Where the gleams and the moth-bitten monsters the
    puddles of soot
And a half-strangled gibbet all cut off an archangel's wings
The flatfooted heart of a memory opened its solitary eye
Till the freak in the showcase was smothered in mucus
    and sweat

A cluster of insane massacres turns green upon the
    highroad
Green as the nadir of a mystery in the closet of a dream
And a wild growth of lascivious pamphlets became a
    beehive
The afternoon scrambles like an asylum out of its hovel
The afternoon swallows a bucketful of chemical sorrows
And the owners of rubber pitchforks bake all their illusions
In an oven of dirty globes and weedgrown stupors

Now the beckoning nudity of diseases putrifies the saloon
The severed limbs of the galaxy wriggle like chambermaids
The sewing-machine on the pillar condenses the windmill's
    halo
Which poisoned the last infanta by placing a tooth in her
    ear
When the creeping groans of the cellar's anemone vanished
The nightmare spun on the roof a chain-armour of
    handcuffs
And the ashtray balanced a ribbon upon a syringe

An opaque whisper flies across the forest
Shaking its trailing sleeves like a steaming spook
Till the icicle stabs at the breast with the bleeding nipple
And bristling pot-hooks slit open the garden's fan
In the midst of the flickering sonorous hemlocks
A screen of hysteria blots out the folded hemlocks
And feathery eyelids conceal the volcano's mouth.

Phenomena

It was during a heat-wave. Someone whose dress seemed to have forgotten who was wearing it appeared to me at the end of a pause in the conversation. She was so adorable that I had to forbid her to pass across my footstool again. Without warning, changing from blue to purple, the night-sky suffered countless meteoric bombardments from the other side of the curtain, and the portcullis fell like an eyelid.

The milk had turned sour in its effort to avoid the centrifugal attraction of a blemish on its own skin. Everything was mounting to the surface. My last hope was to diminish the barometric pressure at least enough to enable me to get out from beneath it alive.

In the end, I remembered that she would not have to make the decision herself, as her own fate was sufficient justification for the hostility of the elements. I turned the page. Nothing could have been more baffling than the way in which the words rose from the places where they had been printed, hovered in the air at a distance of about six inches from my face and finally, without having much more than disturbed my impression of their habitual immobility, dissolved into the growing darkness. As I have said, it was during a heat-wave, and the lightning had well nigh worn itself out in trying to attain the limit of its incandescence. I suddenly forgot what I was supposed to be doing, and the soil beneath my feet loosened itself from the hold of the force of gravity and began to slide gradually downwards, with the sound of a distant explosion.

FROM HÖLDERLIN'S MADNESS

Figure in a Landscape

The verdant valleys full of rivers
Sang a fresh song to the thirsty hills.
The rivers sang:
'Our mother is the Night, into the Day we flow. The mills
Which toil our waters have no thirst. We flow
Like light.'

      And the great birds
Which dwell among the rocks, flew down
Into the dales to drink, and their dark wings
Threw flying shades across the pastures green.

At dawn the rivers flowed into the sea.
The mountain birds
Rose out of sleep like a winged cloud, a single fleet
And flew into a newly-risen sun.

– Anger of the sun: the daily blood-red rays which strike
   oblique
Through olive branches on the slopes and kill the kine.
– Tears of the sun: the summer evening rains which hang
   grey veils
Between the earth and sky, and soak the corn, and brim
   the lakes.

– Dream of the sun: the mists which swim down from the
  icy heights
And hide the gods who wander on the mountain-sides at
  noon.

The sun was anguished, and the sea
Threw up its crested arms and cried aloud out of the
  depths;
And the white horses of the waves raced the black horses
  of the clouds;
The rocky peaks clawed at the sky like gnarled imploring
  hands;
And the black cypresses strained upwards like the sex of a
  hanged man.

                              *

Across the agonizing land there fled
Among the landscape's limbs (the limbs
Of a vast denuded body torn and vanquished from within)
The chaste white road,
Prolonged into the distance like a plaint.

Between the opposition of the night and day
Between the opposition of the earth and sky
Between the opposition of the sea and land
Between the opposition of the landscape and the road
A traveller came
                    Whose only nudity his armour was
Against the whirlwind and the weapon, the undoing
  wound,

And met himself half-way.

Spectre as white as salt in the crude light of the sky
Spectre confronted by flesh, the present and past
Meet timelessly upon the endless road,
Merge timelessly in time and pass away,
Dreamed face away from stricken face into the bourn
Of the unborn, and the real face of age into the fastnesses
    of death.

Infinitely small among the infinitely huge
Drunk with the rising fluids of his breast, his boiling
    heart,
Exposed and naked as the skeleton – upon the knees
Like some tormented desert saint – he flung
The last curse of regret against Omnipotence.
And the lightning struck his face.

*

After the blow, the bruised earth blooms again,
The storm-wrack, wrack of the cloudy sea
Dissolve, the rocks relax,
As the pallid phallus sinks in the clear dawn
Of a new day, and the wild eyes melt and close
And the eye of the sun is no more blind –

Clear milk of love, O lave the devastated vale,
And peace of high-noon, soothe the traveller's pain
Whose hands still grope and clutch, whose head
Thrown back entreats the guerison
And music of your light!

The valley rivers irrigate the land, the mills
Revolve, the hills are fecund with the cypress and the vine,
And the great eagles guard the mountain heights.

Above the peaks in mystery there sit
The Presences, the Unseen in the sky,
Inscrutable, whose influences like rays
Descend upon him, pass through and again
Like golden bees the hive of his lost head.

FROM MISERERE

De Profundis

Out of these depths:

Where footsteps wander in the marsh of death
   and an
Intense infernal glare is on our faces facing down:

Out of these depths, what shamefaced cry
Half choked in the dry throat, as though a stone
Were our confounded tongue, can ever rise:
Because the mind has been struck blind
And may no more conceive
Thy Throne . . .

Because the depths
Are clear with only death's
Marsh-light, because the rock of grief
Is clearly too extreme for us to breath:
Deepen our deaths,

And aid our unbelief.

Kyrie

Is man's destructive lust insatiable? There is
Grief in the blow that shatters the innocent face.
Pain blots out clearer sense. And pleasure suffers
The trial thrust of death in even the bride's embrace.

The black catastrophe that can lay waste our worlds
May be unconsciously desired. Fear masks our face;
And tears as warm and cruelly wrung as blood
Are tumbling even in the mouth of our grimace.

How can our hope ring true? Fatality of guilt
And complicated anguish confounds time and place;
While from the tottering ancestral house an angry voice
Resounds in prophecy. Grant us extraordinary grace,

O spirit hidden in the dark in us and deep,
And bring to light the dream out of our sleep.

Lachrymae

Slow are the years of light:
                  and more immense
Than the imagination. And the years return
Until the Unity is filled. And heavy are
The lengths of Time with the slow weight of tears.
Since Thou didst weep, on a remote hill-side
Beneath the olive-trees, fires of unnumbered stars
Have burnt the years away, until we see them now:
Since Thou didst weep, as many tears
Have flowed like hourglass sand.
Thy tears were all.
And when our secret face
Is blind because of the mysterious
Surging of tears wrung by our most profound
Presentiment of evil in man's fate, our cruellest wounds
Become Thy stigmata. They are Thy tears which fall.

Ecce Homo

Whose is this horrifying face,
This putrid flesh, discoloured, flayed,
Fed on by flies, scorched by the sun?
Whose are these hollow red-filmed eyes
And thorn-spiked head and spear-struck side?
Behold the Man: He is Man's Son.

Forget the legend, tear the decent veil
That cowardice or interest devised
To make their mortal enemy a friend,
To hide the bitter truth all His wounds tell,
Lest the great scandal be no more disguised:
He is in agony till the world's end,

And we must never sleep during that time!
He is suspended on the cross-tree now
And we are onlookers at the crime,
Callous contemporaries of the slow
Torture of God. Here is the hill
Made ghastly by His spattered blood

Whereon He hangs and suffers still:
See, the centurions wear riding-boots,
Black shirts and badges and peaked caps,
Greet one another with raised-arm salutes;
They have cold eyes, unsmiling lips;
Yet these His brothers know not what they do.

And on his either side hang dead
A labourer and a factory hand,

Or one is maybe a lynched Jew
And one a Negro or a Red,
Coolie or Ethiopian, Irishman,
Spaniard or German democrat.

Behind His lolling head the sky
Glares like a fiery cataract
Red with the murders of two thousand years
Committed in His name and by
Crusaders, Christian warriors
Defending faith and property.

Amid the plain beneath His transfixed hands,
Exuding darkness as indelible
As guilty stains, fanned by funereal
And lurid airs, besieged by drifting sands
And clefted landslides our about-to-be
Bombed and abandoned cities stand.

He who wept for Jerusalem
Now sees His prophecy extend
Across the greatest cities of the world,
A guilty panic reason cannot stem
Rising to raze them all as He foretold;
And He must watch this drama to the end.

Though often named, He is unknown
To the dark kingdoms at His feet
Where everything disparages His words,
And each man bears the common guilt alone
And goes blindfolded to his fate,
And fear and greed are sovereign lords.

The turning point of history
Must come. Yet the complacent and the proud
And who exploit and kill, may be denied –
Christ of Revolution and of Poetry –
The resurrection and the life
Wrought by your spirit's blood.

Involved in their own sophistry
The black priest and the upright man
Faced by subversive truth shall be struck dumb,
Christ of Revolution and of Poetry,
While the rejected and condemned become
Agents of the divine.

Not from a monstrance silver-wrought
But from the tree of human pain
Redeem our sterile misery,
Christ of Revolution and of Poetry,
That man's long journey through the night
May not have been in vain.

FROM METAPHYSICAL POEMS
Lowland

Heavy with rain and dense stagnating green
Of old trees guarding tombs these gardens
Sink in the dark and drown. The wet fields run
Together in the middle of the plain. And there are heard
Stampeding herds of horses and a cry,
More long and lamentable as the rains increase,
From out of the beyond.
                                    O dionysian
Desire breaking that voice, released
By fear and torment, out of our lowland rear
A lofty, savage and enduring monument!

Winter Garden

The season's anguish, crashing whirlwind, ice,
Have passed, and cleansed the trodden paths
That silent gardeners have strewn with ash.

The iron circles of the sky
Are worn away by tempest;
Yet in this garden there is no more strife:
The Winter's knife is buried in the earth.
Pure music is the cry that tears
The birdless branches in the wind.
No blossom is reborn. The blue
Stare of the pond is blind.

And no-one sees
A restless stranger through the morning stray
Across the sodden lawn, whose eyes
Are tired of weeping, in whose breast
A savage sun consumes its hidden day.

The Fortress

The socket-free lone visionary eye,
Soaring reflectively
Through regions sealed from macrocosmic light
By inner sky's impenetrable shell,
Often is able to descry:

Beyond the abdominal range's hairless hills
And lunar chasms of the porphyry
Mines; and beyond the forest whose each branch
Bears a lit candle, and the nine
Zigzagging paths which lead into the mind's
Most dangerous far reach; beyond
The calm lymphatic sea
Laving the wound of birth, and the
Red dunes of rot upon its farther shore:

A heaving fortress built up like a breast
Exposed like a huge breast high on its rock.
Streaming with milky brightness, the domed top
Wreathed in irradiant rainbow cloud.
                                    The shock
Of visions stuns the hovering eye, which cannot see
What caverns of deep blood those white walls hide,
Concealing ever rampant underneath
The dark chimera Death-in-life
Defending Life from death.

Dichters Leben

Lodged in a corner of his breast
Like a black hole torn by the loss
Of an ancestral treasure, like a thorn
Implanted ineradicably by his first
Sharp realization of the world, or like a cross
To which his life was to be nailed, he bore
Always the ache of an anxiety, a grief
Which nothing could explain, but which some nights
Would make him cry that he could fight no more.

Time ploughed its way through him; and change
Immersed him in disorder and decay.
Only the strange
Interior ray of the bleak flame
Which charred his heart's core could illuminate
The hidden unity of his life's theme.

He knew how the extremity of night
Can sterilize the final germ of faith;
Appearance crushed him with its steady weight;
Futility discoloured with its breath
His tragic vision. All his strength was spent
In holding to some sense from day to day . . .
Slowly he fell towards dismemberment.

Yet when he lay
At last exhausted under his stilled blood's
Thick cover and eyes' earth-stained lids,

The constant burden of his breast
(Long work of yeast) arose with joy
Into its first full freedom, metamorphosized, released.

Legendary Fragment

Below, in the dark midst, the opened thighs
Gave up their mystery. Myrrh, cassia
And spikenard obscurely emanated from
The inmost blackness. As from all around
There rose a heavy sighing and a troubled light:
Reverberated in the ears and eyes
And stunned the senses.
                           Thus the harlot queen
Was vanquished, while the outmost walls
Of that great town still echoed with her praise.

The Open Tomb

Vibrant with silence is the last sealed room
That fever-quickened breathing cannot break:
Magnetic silence and unshakably doomed breath
Hung like a screen of ice
Between the cavern and the closing eyes,
Between the last day and the final scene
Of death, unwitnessed save by one:

By Omega! the angel whose dark wind
Of wings and trumpet lips
Stirs with disruptive storm the clinging folds
Of stalagmatic foliage lachrymose
Hung from the lofty crypt, where endlessly
The phalanx passes, two by three, with all
The hypnotizing fall of stairs.

Their faces are unraised as yet from sleep;
The pace is slow, and down the steep descent
Their carried candles eddy like a stream;
While on each side, through window in the rock,
Beyond the tunnelled grottoes there are seen
Serene the sunless but how dazzling plains
Where like a sea resounds our open tomb.

The Three Stars

A PROPHECY

The night was Time:
The phases of the moon,
Dynamic influence, controller of the tides,
Its changing face and cycle of quick shades,
Were History, which seemed unending. Then
Occurred the prophesied and the to be
Recounted hour when the reflection ceased
To flow like unseen life-blood in between
The night's tenebral mirror and the lunar light,
Exchanging meaning. Anguish like a crack
Ran with its ruin from the fulfilled Past
Towards the Future's emptiness; and *black*,
Invading all the prism, became absolute.

Black was the No-time at the heart
Of Time (the frameless mirror's back),
But still the Anguish shook
As though with memory and with anticipation: till
Its terror's trembling broke
By an unhoped-for miracle Negation's spell:
Death died and Birth was born with one great cry
And out of some uncharted spaceless sky
Into the new-born night three white stars fell.

And were suspended there a while for all
To see and understand (though none may tell
The inmost meaning of this Mystery).

The first star has a name which stands

For many names of all things that begin
And all first thoughts of undivided minds;
The second star
Is nameless and shines bleakly like the pain
Of an existence conscious only of its end,
And inarticulate, alone
And blind. Immeasurably far
Each from the other first and second spin;
Yet to us at this moment they appear
So close to one another that their rays
In one blurred conflagration intertwine:
So that the third seems born
Of their embracing: till the outer pair
Are separate seen again
Fixed in their true extremes; and in between
These two gleams' hemispheres, unseen
But shining everywhere
The third star balanced shall henceforward burn
Through all dark still to come, serene,
Ubiquitous, immaculately clear;
A magnet in the middle of the maze, to draw us on
Towards that Bethlehem beyond despair
Where from the womb of Nothing shall be born
A Son.

FROM PERSONAL POEMS

The Fabulous Glass

In my deep Mirror's blindest heart
A Cone I planted there to sprout.
Sprang up a Tree tall as a cloud
And each branch bore a loud-voiced load
Of Birds as bright as their own song;
But when a distant death-knell rang
My Tree fell down, and where it lay
A Centipede disgustingly
Swarmed its quick length across the ground!
Thick shadows fell inside my mind;
Until an Alcove rose to view
In which, obscure at first, there now
Appeared a Virgin and her Child;
But it was horrid to behold
How she consumed that Infant's Face
With her voracious Mouth. Her Dress
Was Black, and blotted all out. Then
A phosphorescent Triple Chain
Of Pearls against the darkness hung
Like a Temptation; but ere long
They vanished, leaving in their place
A Peacock, which lit up the glass
By opening his Fan of Eyes:
And thus closed down my Self-regarding Gaze.

Apologia

'Poète et non honnête homme.'
PASCAL

1

It's not the Age,
Disease, or accident, but sheer
Perversity (or so one must suppose),
That pins me to the singularly bare
Boards of this trestle-stage
That I have mounted to adopt the pose
Of a demented wrestler, with gorge full
Of phlegm, eyes bleared with salt, and knees
Knocking like ninepins: a most furious fool!

2

Fixed by the nib
Of an inept pen to a bleak page
Before the glassy gaze of a ghost mob,
I stand once more to face the silent rage
Of my unseen Opponent, and begin
The same old struggle for the doubtful prize:
Each stanza is a round, and every line
A blow aimed at the too elusive chin
Of that Oblivion which cannot fail to win.

3

Before I fall
Down silent finally, I want to make
One last attempt at utterance, and tell
How my absurd desire was to compose
A single poem with my mental eyes

Wide open, and without even one lapse
From that most scrupulous Truth which I pursue
When not pursuing Poetry. – Perhaps
Only the poem I can never write is *true*.

[THREE]

1943–1950

The Second Coming

In the dream theatre, my seat was on the balcony, and the
auditorium had been partly converted into an extension of
the stage. Several little Italia Conti girls ran forward past
my seat from somewhere behind me, and one of them
clambered over a ledge and seemed to fall (she must have
been suspended by a wire) to the floor below. She gave a
small scream: 'God is born!' On a little nest of straw on the
ground close to where she had fallen, a baby doll suddenly
appeared. At the same moment, a hideous scarecrow-like
Svengali-Rasputin figure, mask larger than life-size and
painted like an evil clown in a Chagall apocalypse, playing an
enormous violin which somehow contrived also to suggest
the scythe of Father Time, rose upon the circular dais in the
centre of the auditorium. I realized at once that he was the
personification of Sin and Death. 'When I play my tune,
there is not a single one of you all who does not join the
dance!' I was most painfully moved by the strident yet
cajoling music and by the knowledge that what he had said
was nothing less than the truth. Everything then began to
move around confusingly. On the darkened stage, thick
black gauze curtains had lifted, and one saw a squat black
cross outlined against a streak of haggard white storm light
across the back-cloth sky. Finally, the stage was full of
menacing, jerkily swaying bogies, thick black distorted
crucifixes with white slit eyes, covered with newspaper
propaganda headlines, advancing towards the audience like
a ju-ju ceremonial dance of medicine men. At the very end of

the performance, a clearly ringing voice, representing the light which must increasingly prevail against these figures, cried: 'All propaganda that is not true Christian revolutionary propaganda is sickness and falsehood!'

After Twenty Springs

How vehemently and with what primavernal fire
Has there been voiced the seasonal conviction that new
    birth,
Aurora, revolution, resurrection from the dead,
Palingenesia, was about to be, was near,
Must surely come. Of course it shall, it must.
The bones shall live, the dust awake and sing.
I hope and trust I shall be there. But seriously,
If it has not already come, and it is we
Who lack the faith to recognize it, if the sun
That shone upon the just and unjust does not shine
This spring upon the risen dead, then what a long
Business this getting born again must be. We dead
Are living, really; and the living are asleep,
Lawrence; and gladly in their sleep they read
The Twentieth Anniversary reprint of your writings,
    stirred
Fitfully for a while to more impassioned dream.
For many love you now, Redbeard, and wish you had not
    died
In bitterness, before your time. On dead man's isle,
We who survived you and are struggling still to-day
(If very feebly and unostentatiously)
For life, more life, new life, fine warm full-blooded life,
Are reconciled with patience, on commemorating you.

[FOUR]

1951–1968

Elegiac Improvisation on the Death of Paul Eluard

A tender mouth a sceptical shy mouth
A firm fastidious slender mouth
A Gallic mouth an asymmetrical mouth

He opened his mouth he spoke without hesitation
He sat down and wrote as he spoke without changing a
   word
And the words that he wrote still continue to speak with
   his mouth:

Warmly and urgently
Simply, convincingly
Gently and movingly
Softly, sincerely
Clearly, caressingly
Bitterly, painfully
Pensively, stumblingly
Brokenly, heartbreakingly
Uninterruptedly
In clandestinity
In anguish, in arms and in anger,
In passion, in Paris, in person
In partisanship, as the poet

Of France's Resistance, the spokesman
Of unconquerable free fraternity.

And now his printed words all add up to a sum total
And it can be stated he wrote just so many poems
And the commentators like undertakers take over
The task of annotating his complete collected works.
Yet the discursivity of the void
Diverts and regales the whole void then re-enters the void
While every printed page is a swinging door
Through which one can pass in either of two directions
On one's way towards oblivion
And from the blackness looming through the doorway
The burning bush of hyperconsciousness
Can fill the vacuum abhorred by human nature
And magic images flower from the poet's speech
He said, 'There is nothing that I regret,
I still advance,' and he advances
He passes us Hyperion passes on
Prismatic presence
A light broken up into colours whose rays pass from him
To friends in solitude, leaves of as many branches
As a single and solid solitary trunk has roots
Just as so many sensitive lines cross each separate leaf
On each of the far-reaching branches of sympathy's tree
Now the light of the prism has flashed like a bird down
    the dark-blue grove
At the end of which mountains of shadow pile up beyond
    sight
Oh radiant prism
A wing has been torn and its feathers drift scattered by
    flight.

Yet still from the dark through the door shines the poet's
    mouth speaking
In rain as in fine weather
The climate of his speaking
Is silence, calm and sunshine,
Sublime cloudburst and downpour,
The changing wind that breaks out blows away
All words – wind that is mystery
Wind of the secret spirit
That breaks up words' blind weather
With radiant breath of Logos
When silence is a falsehood
And all things no more named
Like stones flung into emptiness
Fall down through bad eternity
All things fall out and drop down, fall away
If no sincere mouth speaks
To recreate the world
Alone in the world it may be
The only candid mouth
Truth's sole remaining witness
Disinterested, distinct, undespairing mouth
'Inspiring mouth still more than a mouth inspired'
Speaking still in all weathers
Speaking to all those present
As he speaks to us here at present
Speaks to the man at the bar and the girl on the staircase
The flowerseller, the newspaper woman, the student
The foreign lady wearing a shawl in the faubourg
    garden
The boy with a bucket cleaning the office windows
The friendly fellow in charge of the petrol station
The sensitive cynical officer thwarting description

Like the well-informed middle-class man who prefers to
    remain undescribed
And the unhappy middle-aged woman who still hopes and
    cannot be labelled
The youth who's rejected all words that could ever be
    spoken
To conceal and corrupt where they ought to reveal what
    they name.

The truth that lives eternally is told in time
The laughing beasts the landscape of delight
The sensuality of noon the tranquil midnight
The vital fountains the heroic statues
The barque of youth departing for Cytheria
The ruined temples and the blood of sunset
The banks of amaranth the bower of ivy
The storms of spring and autumn's calm are Now
Absence is only of all that is not Now
And all that is true is and is here Now
The flowers the fruit the green fields and the snow's field
The serpent dance of the silver ripples of dawn
The shimmering breasts the tender hands are present
The open window looks out on the realm of Now
Whose vistas glisten with leaves and immaculate clouds
And Now all beings are seen to become more wonderful
More radiant more intense and are now more naked
And more awake and in love and in need of love
Life dreamed is now life lived, unlived life realized
The lucid moment, the lifetime's understanding
Become reconciled and at last surpassed by Now
Words spoken by one man awake in a sleeping crowd
Remain with their unique vibration's still breathing
    enigma

When the crowd has dispersed and the poet who spoke
has gone home.

PAUL ELUARD has come back to his home the
world.

FROM NIGHT THOUGHTS

2. *Megalometropolitan Carnival*

[*Narration One*]
Enter the Dreams.

[*Narration Two*]
The Dreams enter the City.
Drifting in swiftly twisting clouds above the roofs,
Their whirling fever-coloured smoke crosses the moon;
As they race past, its contours blur and tremble.
A moment after, real clouds blot its face.

[*Narration One*]
Enter the Dream.

[*Narration Two*]
Enter the Dream's great glimmering park.
Only at first is it still dead of night.
Slide softly, stepping rapidly, at first.
Here there still lingers a strange stealth and stillness.
The beams that fill the early dreams are soft as twilight
In the first place. In this faint light you must move swift
    as swimmers,
Move with short strokes beneath the lowslung boughs,
The grey, long-bearded, overhanging branches
Of ancient trees still lining all these avenues.
You'll have to hurry down these thoroughfares,
Though splendid shops and gardens catch your eye.
All signposts point in only one direction.

[*Narration One*]
Follow the fingers, you can't lose your way,

It won't take long to reach the central space,
That is the special place you have to find.
Just one street further. Here at last you are.

[*Narration Two*]
Here is the Circus in the Square that represents
The very heart of the primeval City. Now's the time
To recollect that you've received a secret summons
To a rendezvous with the Unknown, at the foot of the
    Fountain
That leaps without spray, a thin glimmering quicksilver
    pillar,
Above the memorial marking the first fatal spot,
The meeting place of the First Person with Persons
    Unnamed
At the heart of the Forest that grew where the City now
    stands.

[*Narration Three*]
The quicksilver Fountain that's hovering there like a
    column allures
All who enter the lair of the Labyrinth-Omphalos Boss,
Whose domain lies beneath, in the earth. Yet if anyone
    nears
The basin too closely, at once it will sink underground.
By the time you've got right to the axis round which the
    square circles,
You will find that it's no longer there.

[*Narration One*]
Just stand still for a moment. No need to be scared.
Pay no heed to the thunder of traffic, the dazzle of lights
On the walls flashing messages round you on every side.

Soon, just where the Fountain has vanished, the earth at
   your feet,
At the heart of empirical hubbub, will yawn open wide
And the cavernous Subway's mouth show you the way
   down inside.

[*Narration Two*]
Now you follow the steps and descend to the City's true
   heart,
And are soon in a Plaza illumined more brightly than day
Where more people are hurrying in all directions than up
   there above.
Close at hand is the brisk business district, just under you
   lies
The platform from which the incessant electric expresses
Go rushing from City to faraway Suburbs, and back from
   the Suburbs again.

[*Narration Three*]
Here are underground Boulevards bright with Bazaars,
   here you'll find
Vast fields for the shop-window gazer to graze in, Arcades
Branch off on each side, endless Galleries lined with
   glasscases invite
To inspection of carloads of diamondmine loot, of forests
   of flowers,
Tropic fruits piled in tiers, Pin-up waxwork girls posed
   in parades
To show off new nylons, new sequins, new rhinestones,
   new lace-trimmed furcoats.

[*Narration One*]
But don't linger too long for a rush-hour approaches and
   here it's unwise

To risk getting caught by the tide of the throng that flows
    through at its height.
Better make your way now to the flights of steps all
    leading down
To the slow-moving staircases, up to the fast escalators
Descending past columns of spiralling stairs to the level
    where tubes
Have been bored for the feet to press through from the
    foot of one flight

    [*Narration Two*]
Of stepping stones, on to the passages in, then the
    passages out,
To the thoroughfares out of which more escalators are
    moving, some more
Slowly, the others more quickly, first up and then down,
    on and on,
On and off, up and up, down down down, go on down,
    till at last
The wonderful system will crown the true will to success
    with success
As the peace known at zero-hour's peak on the heart of
    the rusher descends.

    [*Guide Voice*]
As you move at a pace that gets constantly faster, your
    eyes
Are increasingly caught and held fast at each step by one
    after
Another phrase, slogan and image set up to solicit as much
Of the crowd-individual's attention as each in his hurry
    can spare.

[*Narration One*]

You may look where you like for the public's fastidious
    and only permits
Its favourite posters to brighten the walls of such sanctums
    as these:
Now the principal stations afford a great treat with the
    constant variety
Of the attractions inviting the traveller's mind's eye to
    rove towards
All sorts of model resorts; at his journey's end wait to
    stare down on him
On his arrival more posters depicting the places abroad
    he must
Hasten to visit as soon as he can to discover:

[*Narration Two*]

NEW VISTAS NEW THRESHOLDS NEW PLEASURES
    NEW BEAUTIES NEW BEACHES NEW LIGHT
ON OLD-WORLD INNS NEW WORLDS IN DISGUISE
    OLD CATHEDRALS SPOTLIGHTED
NEW CRUISES TO BEAUTYSPOTS SEA-COASTS BEST
    SUITED TO NUDES

[*Narration Three*]

Look! Here posters plaster the best people's eye with
    huge glimpses
Of Scenes from the Very Best Shows of the Year by the
    Star-Chamber
Critics' Assembly Selected: The Most Highly Praised,
    the Best Advertised, then
The most Noted for Highlypaid Acting, the Most
    Controversial,
The Brightest, the Loudest, Most Daringly Brutal, and
    Quite the Most Crude.

[*Narration One*]

The Crowd's hardheaded leaders alone have the leisure to
cast a glance over them

As they press past down the passage from exit to
box-office queue but they turn

To present to the next passerby their opinion for what it
is worth and

He'll then in his turn send it on to be sent on till common
consent

Has agreed that it's fit to be fully divulged to the public
at large.

[*Narration Two*]

Now here you must follow the people in front of you
down some more stairs

Where as you descend you will find on each side are
arranged on the walls

More advertisements eager to snatch at your glance as
you pass:

If you miss one or two it won't matter, you'll find them
again further on

[*Publicity Chorus*]

STRAPLESS BREASTAPPEAL BRA MAKES YOU
HARDER TO GET

NEW LYNX LIMOUSINE WITH LOW FAMILY EYELINE

DON'T LET THEM DESCRIBE YOU AS DIRTY! GET
'WET'

HOW'S YOUR COLON LOOK? TREAT IT TO
LIQUORICE SOAP

WATCH APPROACH OF PHENOMENAL NEW STAR
ON SKYLINE

VAN WORMWOOD EXCLUSIVELY FEATURED IN
'DOPE'

'THIS SOULTWISTER BLISTERS THE PAINT OFF
THE SET!'
DRINK MORE DRINK! WEAR MORE CLOTHES!
DON'T LOSE HOPE! DON'T FORGET!
WEAR MORE SMILES PLEASE! LAUGH LOUDER!
LOOK AFTER YOURSELF!
USE CHARM AND DISCRETION! BE TOUGH! DON'T
GET LAID ON THE SHELF!

[Train-Wheels Chorus]
I couldn't care less I couldn't care less I couldn't care less I
couldn't
A chance you can't afford to lose a chance you can't afford to lose a
Smooth as glass and tough as hell as smooth as glass and tough as
hell
The damned are the damned are the damned are the damned are the
The World to come the Atom Plan the World of Man the
Atom Bomb the
Coming Day the Biggest Bang the Wrath of God the Atom Age
the Day of Wrath . . . (ad inf.)

Part of a Poem in Progress

STROPHE I

Our gentle sister Memory,
Our brother Brute Desire,
Conspire from time to time in Time
To set the World afire.

They never can destroy this world,
The strange incestuous Pair;
Their loving intercourse takes place
Within their Father's care.

Their Father is a whoring man,
Although his hair is grey.
He will not set his scythe aside
Till he has had his play.

He loves his fornicating Twins,
He loves to watch them sin;
But hammers at the window-pane,
And breaks out once he's in:

'How dare you break my sacred laws!
How many times a day
Have I had to repeat to you
What all the Great Books say:

'There is a limit to all things:
Thou canst not but comply.
What I have told you once for all
Thou shalt believe or die.

'You shall not suffer in your bed,
But only in the Bath
Which I am going to prepare
As for an aftermath.

'This afternoon, before the Sun
Has trod his wearying way
Toward his final resting-place,
You shall resume your play.

'But first I'll strip you to the bone
To see in what clean dew
You have been washing in like snow
No spring rains can renew.

'There *is* a mighty Mystery,
In spite of your belief
That Time and old Eternity
Were nothing but a grief.

'The griefs that come, the joys that go,
The vague material things,
Are nothing to the forms of me
Our greater Future brings.

'So get you ready for the Bath
Of Blood you're going to take,
Since, as I happened to pass by,
I saw your Great Mistake.'

W. S. GRAHAM

W. S. GRAHAM

The Beast in the Space

Shut up. Shut up. There's nobody here.
If you think you hear somebody knocking
On the other side of the words, pay
No attention. It will be only
The great creature that thumps its tail
On silence on the other side.
If you do not even hear that
I'll give the beast a quick skelp
And through Art you'll hear it yelp.

The beast that lives on silence takes
Its bite out of either side.
It pads and sniffs between us. Now
It comes and laps my meaning up.
Call it over. Call it across
This curious, necessary space.
Get off, you terrible inhabiter
Of silence. I'll not have it. Get
Away to whoever it is will have you.

He's gone and if he's gone to you
That's fair enough. For on this side
Of the words it's late. The heavy moth
Bangs on the pane. The whole house
Is sleeping and I remember
I am not here, only the space
I sent the terrible beast across.
Watch. He bites. Listen gently
To any song he snorts or growls
And give him food. He means neither
Well or ill towards you. Above
All, shut up. Give him your love.

Malcolm Mooney's Land

I

Today, Tuesday, I decided to move on
Although the wind was veering. Better to move
Than have them at my heels, poor friends
I buried earlier under the printed snow.
From wherever it is I urge these words
To find their subtle vents, the northern dazzle
Of silence cranes to watch. Footprint on foot
Print, word on word and each on a fool's errand.
Malcolm Mooney's Land. Elizabeth
Was in my thoughts all morning and the boy.
Wherever I speak from or in what particular
Voice, this is always a record of me in you.
I can record at least out there to the west
The grinding bergs and, listen, further off
Where we are going, the glacier calves
Making its sudden momentary thunder.
This is as good a night, a place as any.

II

From the rimed bag of sleep, Wednesday,
My words crackle in the early air.
Thistles of ice about my chin,
My dreams, my breath a ruff of crystals.
The new ice falls from canvas walls.
O benign creature with the small ear-hole,
Submerger under silence, lead
Me where the unblubbered monster goes
Listening and makes his play.
Make my impediment mean no ill
And be itself a way.

A fox was here last night (Maybe Nansen's,
Reading my instruments.) the prints
All round the tent and not a sound.
Not that I'd have him call my name.
Anyhow how should he know? Enough
Voices are with me here and more
The further I go. Yesterday
I heard the telephone ringing deep
Down in a blue crevasse.
I did not answer it and could
Hardly bear to pass.

Landlice, always my good bedfellows
Ride with me in my sweaty seams.
Come bonny friendly beasts, brother
To the grammarsow and the word-louse,
Bite me your presence, keep me awake
In the cold with work to do, to remember
To put down something to take back.
I have reached the edge of earshot here
And by the laws of distance
My words go through the smoking air
Changing their tune on silence.

III

My friend who loves owls
Has been with me all day
Walking at my ear
And speaking of old summers
When to speak was easy.
His eyes are almost gone
Which made him hear well.
Under our feet the great

Glacier drove its keel.
What is to read there
Scored out in the dark?

Later the north-west distance
Thickened towards us.
The blizzard grew and proved
Too filled with other voices
High and desperate
For me to hear him more.
I turned to see him go
Becoming shapeless into
The shrill swerving snow.

IV

Today, Friday, holds the white
Paper up too close to see
Me here in a white-out in this tent of a place.
And why is it there has to be
Some place to find, however momentarily
To speak from, some distance to listen to?

Out at the far-off edge I hear
Colliding voices, drifted, yes,
To find me through the slowly opening leads.
Tomorrow I'll try the rafted ice.
Have I not been trying to use the obstacle
Of language well? It freezes round us all.

V

Why did you choose this place
For us to meet? Sit
With me between this word

And this, my furry queen.
Yet not mistake this
For the real thing. Here
In Malcolm Mooney's Land
I have heard many
Approachers in the distance
Shouting. Early hunters
Skittering across the ice
Full of enthusiasm
And making fly and,
Within the ear, the yelling
Spear steepening to
The real prey, the right
Prey of the moment.
The honking choir in fear
Leave the tilting floe
And enter the sliding water.
Above the bergs the foolish
Voices are lighting lamps
And all their sounds make
This diary of a place,
Writing us both in.

Come and sit. Or is
It right to stay here
While, outside the tent
The bearded blinded go
Calming their children
Into the ovens of frost?
And what's the news? What
Brought you here through
The spring leads opening?

Elizabeth, you and the boy
Have been with me often
Especially on those last
Stages. Tell him a story.
Tell him I came across
An old sulphur bear
Sawing his log of sleep
Loud beneath the snow.
He puffed the powdered light
Up on to this page
And here his reek fell
In splinters among
These words. He snored well.
Elizabeth, my furry
Pelted queen of Malcolm
Mooney's Land, I made
You here beside me
For a moment out
Of the correct fatigue.
I have made myself alone now.
Outside the tent endless
Drifting hummock crests.
Words drifting on words.
The real unabstract snow.

I Leave This at Your Ear

FOR NESSIE DUNSMUIR

I leave this at your ear for when you wake,
A creature in its abstract cage asleep.
Your dreams blindfold you by the light they make.

The owl called from the naked-woman tree
As I came down by the Kyle farm to hear
Your house silent by the speaking sea.

I have come late but I have come before
Later with slaked steps from stone to stone
To hope to find you listening for the door.

I stand in the ticking room. My dear, I take
A moth kiss from your breath. The shore gulls cry.
I leave this at your ear for when you wake.

Letter I

Welcome then anytime. Fare
Well as your skill's worth,
You able-handed sea-blade
Aglint with the inlaid
Scales of the herring host
And hosting light. Good morning
Said that. And that morning
Opened and fairly rose
Keeping sea-pace with us
Sailed out on the long kyle.
Early there I could tell
Under the scaling light
The nerves of each sheared knot
Keelcleft twisting back
Astern to make the wake,
And I saw my death flash
For an instant white like a fish
In the second-sighted sea.

That death is where I lie
In this sea you inherit.
There is no counter to it.

Taken my dear as heir
To yes again the ever
Arriving sea, I wave
Us here out on the move.
May we both fare well through
This difficult element we
Hear welcome in. Farewell
Gives us ever away

To a better host. See, I
Hack steps on the water never
For one lull still but over
Flowing all ways I make
My ways. Always I make
My ways. And as you listen
Here at the felling bow
I'll be myself in vain
Always. Dear you who walk

Your solitude on these
Words, walk their silences
Hearing a morning say
A welcome I have not heard
In words I have not made.

And the good morning rose
Fairly over the bows
And whitely waving fray.
We hauled the nets. And all
That live and silver causeway
Heaving came to our side.

These words said welcome. Fare
Them well from what they are.

Letter IV

Night winked and endeared
Itself to language. Huge
Over the dark verge sauntered
Half the moon. Then all
Its shoal attending stared
Down on the calm and mewing
Firth and in a bright
Breath that night became
You in these words fondly
Through me. Even becomes
Us now. And casts me always
Through who I thought I was.
May Love not cast us out.

Know me by the voice
That speaks outside my choice
And speaks our double breath
Into this formal death.

My dear, here and happy
We are cast off away
Swanning through the slow
Shallows and shearing into
The first heave of the deep
Sea's lusty founds.
And out. Lie here happy
Here on this bed of nets.
Loosen the blouse of night.
It seems no time since we
Lay down to let Love pass.
Past? For almost I stoop

Backward to pick Love up,
From where? My dear, all
You've had of me is always
Here. Lean here. Listen.
Though it is always going.
Nor does it say even
A part, but something else.
Time lowers it into bookmould
Filled with words that lied
To where they came from and
To where they went. Yet, lean
On your elbow here. Listen.

What a great way. So bright.
O the sea is meadowsweet.
That voice talking? It's from
Some family famous for
The sea. There's drink in it.
Where did he drown from, taken
By the sea's barbaric hooks?
Yet lie here, love. Listen
To that voice on the swell
(Old rogue with a skilful keel).
It is that voice which hears
The dog whelk's whimper
And the cockle's call come up
From the deep beds under
Those breaking prisms of water.
And hears old Mooney call Time
Bogtongued like doomsday over
The bar and hears Mooney's
Hanging lamp lapping
The sweet oil from its bowl.

And each word, 'this' and 'this'
Is that night and your breath
Dying on mine moved out
On always the sea moving
Neither its help nor comfort
Between us. Be held a while.

Old Calum's there. Listen.
This is his song he says,
To pass the time at the tiller.
He's sad drunk. Let him be.
He'll not see, that poor
Harper, bat-blind, stone-daft
(That cough was aconite).
Let him go on. His harp's
Some strung breastbone but sweet.
It's often enough their habit,
The old and answered not.

Then what a fine upstander
I was for the cause of Love
And what a fine woman's
Man I went sauntering as.

I could sing a tear out of
The drunk or sober or deaf.
My love would lie pleasanter
Than ever she lay before.

Now she who younger lay
Lies lost in the husk of night.
My far my vanished dears
All in your bowers.

Fondly from a beyond
His song moved to my hand
And moves as you move now.
Yet here's the long heave
To move us through. Say
After me here. 'Unto
My person to be peer.'
And all holds us in the hull
That slides between the waving
Gates and the bow drives
Headlong through the salt
Thicket of the maiden sea.

And shall for Christsake always
Bleed down that streaming door.

Letter VI

A day the wind was hardly
Shaking the youngest frond
Of April I went on
The high moor we know.
I put my childhood out
Into a cocked hat
And you moving the myrtle
Walked slowly over.
A sweet clearness became.
The Clyde sleeved in its firth
Reached and dazzled me.
I moved and caught the sweet
Courtesy of your mouth.
My breath to your breath.
And as you lay fondly
In the crushed smell of the moor
The courageous and just sun
Opened its door.
And there we lay halfway
Your body and my body
On the high moor. Without
A word then we went
Our ways. I heard the moor
Curling its cries far
Across the still loch.

The great verbs of the sea
Come down on us in a roar.
What shall I answer for?

The Constructed Space

Meanwhile surely there must be something to say.
Maybe not suitable but at least happy
In a sense here between us two whoever
We are. Anyhow here we are and never
Before have we two faced each other who face
Each other now across this abstract scene
Stretching between us. This is a public place
Achieved against subjective odds and then
Mainly an obstacle to what I mean.

It is like that remember. It is like that
Very often at the beginning till we are met
By some intention risen up out of nothing.
And even then we know what we are saying
Only when it is said and fixed and dead.
Or maybe, surely, of course we never know
What we have said, what lonely meanings are read
Into the space we make. And yet I say
This silence here for in it I might hear you.

I say this silence or, better, construct this space
So that somehow something may move across
The caught habits of language to you and me.
From where we are it is not us we see
And times are hastening yet, disguise is mortal.
The times continually disclose our home.
Here in the present tense disguise is mortal.
The trying times are hastening. Yet here I am
More truly now this abstract act become.

The Voyages of Alfred Wallis

Worldhauled, he's grounded on God's great bank,
Keelheaved to Heaven, waved into boatfilled arms,
Falls his homecoming leaving that old sea testament,
Watching the restless land sail rigged alongside
Townful of shallows, gulls on the sailing roofs.
And he's heaved once and for all a high dry packet
Pecked wide by curious years of a ferreting sea,
His poor house blessed by very poverty's religious
Breakwater, his past house hung in foreign galleries.
He's that stone sailor towering out of the cupboarding sea
To watch the black boats rigged by a question quietly
Ghost home and ask right out the jackets of oil
And standing white of the crew 'what hellward harbour
Bows down her seawalls to arriving home at last?'

Falls into home his prayerspray. He's there to lie
Seagreat and small, contrary and rare as sand.
Oils overcome and keep his inward voyage.
An Ararat shore, loud limpet stuck to its terror,
Drags home the bible keel from a returning sea
And four black, shouting steerers stationed on movement
Call out arrival over the landgreat houseboat.
The ship of land with birds on seven trees
Calls out farewell like Melville talking down on
Nightfall's devoted barque and the parable whale.
What shipcry falls? The holy families of foam
Fall into wilderness and 'over the jasper sea'.
The gulls wade into silence. What deep seasaint
Whispered this keel out of its element?

The Dark Dialogues

I

I always meant to only
Language swings away
Further before me.

Language swings away
Before me as I go
With again the night rising
Up to accompany me
And that other fond
Metaphor, the sea.
Images of night
And the sea changing
Should know me well enough.

Wanton with riding lights
And staring eyes, Europa
And her high meadow bull
Fall slowly their way
Behind the blindfold and
Across this more or less
Uncommon place.

And who are you and by
What right do I waylay
You where you go there
Happy enough striking
Your hobnail in the dark?
Believe me I would ask
Forgiveness but who
Would I ask forgiveness from?

I speak across the vast
Dialogues in which we go
To clench my words against
Time or the lack of time
Hoping that for a moment
They will become for me
A place I can think in
And think anything in,
An aside from the monstrous.

And this is no other
Place than where I am,
Here turning between
This word and the next.
Yet somewhere the stones
Are wagging in the dark
And you, whoever you are,
That I am other to,
Stand still by the glint
Of the dyke's sparstone,
Because always language
Is where the people are.

II

Almost I, yes, I hear
Huge in the small hours
A man's step on the stair
Climbing the pipeclayed flights
And then stop still
Under the stairhead gas
At the lonely tenement top.
The broken mantle roars
Or dims to a green murmur.

One door faces another.
Here, this is the door
With the loud grain and the name
Unreadable in brass.
Knock, but a small knock,
The children are asleep.
I sit here at the fire
And the children are there
And in this poem I am,
Whoever elsewhere I am,
Their mother through his mother.
I sit with the gas turned
Down and time knocking
Somewhere through the wall.
Wheesht, children, and sleep
As I break the raker up,
It is only the stranger
Hissing in the grate.
Only to speak and say
Something, little enough,
Not out of want
Nor out of love, to say
Something and to hear
That someone has heard me.
This is the house I married
Into, a room and kitchen
In a grey tenement,
The top flat of the land,
And I hear them breathe and turn
Over in their sleep
As I sit here becoming
Hardly who I know.
I have seen them hide

And seek and cry come out
Come out whoever you are
You're not het I called
And called across the wide
Wapenschaw of water.
But the place moved away
Beyond the reach of any
Word. Only the dark
Dialogues drew their breath.
Ah how bright the mantel
Brass shines over me.
Black-lead at my elbow,
Pipe-clay at my feet.
Wheesht and go to sleep
And grow up but not
To say mother mother
Where are the great games
I grew up quick to play.

III

Now in the third voice
I am their father through
Nothing more than where
I am made by this word
And this word to occur.
Here I am makeshift made
By artifice to fall
Upon a makeshift time.
But I can't see. I can't
See in the bad light
Moving (Is it moving?)
Between your eye and mine.
Who are you and yet

It doesn't matter only
I thought I heard somewhere
Someone else walking.
Where are the others? Why,
If there is any other,
Have they gone so far ahead?
Here where I am held
With the old rainy oak
And Cartsburn and the Otter's
Burn aroar in the dark
I try to pay for my keep.
I speak as well as I can
Trying to teach my ears
To learn to use their eyes
Even only maybe
In the end to observe
The behaviour of silence.
Who is it and why
Do you walk here so late
And how should you know to take
The left or the right fork
Or the way where, as a boy,
I used to lie crouched
Deep under the flailing
Boughs of the roaring wood?
Or I lay still
Listening while a branch
Squeaked in the resinous dark
And swaying silences.

Otherwise I go
Only as a shell
Of my former self.

I go with my foot feeling
To find the side of the road,
My head inclined, my ears
Feathered to every wind
Blown between the dykes.
The mist is coming home.
I hear the blind horn
Mourning from the firth.
The big wind blows
Over the shore of my child-
Hood in the off-season.
The small wind remurmurs
The fathering tenement
And a boy I knew running
The hide and seeking streets.
Or do these winds
In their forces blow
Between the words only?

I am the shell held
To Time's ear and you
May hear the lonely leagues
Of the kittiwake and the fulmar.

IV

Or I am always only
Thinking is this the time
To look elsewhere to turn
Towards what was it
I put myself out
Away from home to meet?
Was it this only? Surely
It is more than these words

See on my side
I went halfway to meet.
And there are other times.
But the times are always
Other and now what I meant
To say or hear or be
Lies hidden where exile
Too easily beckons.
What if the terrible times
Moving away find
Me in the end only
Staying where I am always
Unheard by a fault.

So to begin to return
At last neither early
Nor late and go my way
Somehow home across
This gesture become
Inhabited out of hand.
I stop and listen over
My shoulder and listen back
On language for that step
That seems to fall after
My own step in the dark.

Always must be the lost
Or where we turn, and all
For a sight of the dark again.
The farthest away, the least
To answer back come nearest.

And this place is taking

Its time from us though these
Two people or voices
Are not us nor has
The time they seem to move in
To do with what we think
Our own times are. Even
Where they are is only
This one inhuman place.
Yet somewhere a stone
Speaks and maybe a leaf
In the dark turns over.
And whoever I meant
To think I had met
Turns away further
Before me blinded by
This word and this word.

See how presently
The bull and the girl turn
From what they seemed to say,
And turn there above me
With that star-plotted head
Snorting on silence.
The legend turns. And on
Her starry face descried
Faintly astonishment.
The formal meadow fades
Over the ever-widening
Firth and in their time
That not unnatural pair
Turn slowly home.

This is no other place

Than where I am, between
This word and the next.
Maybe I should expect
To find myself only
Saying that again
Here now at the end.
Yet over the great
Gantries and cantilevers
Of love, a sky, real and
Particular, is slowly
Startled into light.

The Thermal Stair

(IN MEMORY OF PETER LANYON)

I called today, Peter, and you were away.
I look out over Botallack and over Ding
Dong and Levant and over the jasper sea.

Find me a thermal to speak and soar to you from
Over Lanyon Quoit and the circling stones standing
High on the moor over Gurnard's Head where some

Time three foxglove summers ago, you came.
The days are shortening over Little Parc Owles.
The poet or painter steers his life to maim

Himself somehow for the job. His job is Love
Imagined into words or paint to make
An object that will stand and will not move.

Peter, I called and you were away, speaking
Only through what you made and at your best.
Look, there above Botallack, the buzzard riding

The salt updraught slides off the broken air
And out of sight to quarter a new place.
The Celtic sea, the Methodist sea is there.

You said once in the Engine
House below Morvah
That words make their world
In the same way as the painter's
Mark surprises him
Into seeing new.

Sit here on the sparstone
In this ruin where
Once the early beam
Engine pounded and broke
The air with industry.

Now the chuck of daws
And the listening sea.

'Shall we go down' you said
'Before the light goes
And stand below the old
Tin-workings around
Morvah and St Just?'
You said 'Here is the sea
Made by alfred wallis
Or any poet or painter's
Eye it encounters.
Or is it better made
By all those vesselled men
Sometime it maintained?
We all make it again.'

Give me your hand, Peter,
To steady me on the word.

Seventy-two by sixty,
Italy hangs on the wall.
A woman stands with a drink
In some polite place
And looks at SARACINESCO
And turns to mention space.
That one if she could

Would ride Artistically
The thermals you once rode.

Peter, the phallic boys
Begin to wink their lights.
Godrevy and the Wolf
Are calling Opening Time.
We'll take the quickest way
The tin singers made.
Climb here where the hand
Will not grasp on air.
And that dark-suited man
Has set the dominoes out
On the Queen's table.
Peter, we'll sit and drink
And go in the sea's roar
To Labrador with Wallis
Or rise on Lanyon's stair.

Uneasy, lovable man, give me your painting
Hand to steady me taking the word-road home.
Lanyon, why is it you're earlier away?
Remember me wherever you listen from.
Lanyon, dingdong dingdong from carn to carn.
It seems tonight all Closing bells are tolling
Across the Duchy shire wherever I turn.

Hilton Abstract

Roger, whether the tree is made
To speak or stand as a tree should,
Lifting its branches over lovers
And moving as the wind moves,
It is the longed-for, loved event,
To be by another aloneness loved.

Hell with this and hell with that
And hell with all the scunnering lot.
This can go and that can go
And leave us with the quick and slow.
And quick and slow are nothing much.
We either touch or do not touch.

Yet the great humilities
Keep us always ill at ease.
The weather moves above us and
The mouse makes its little sound.
Whatever happens happens and
The false hands are moving round.

Hell with this and hell with that.
All that's best is better not.
Yet the great humilities
Keep us always ill at ease,
And in keeping us they go
Through the quick and through the slow.

The Soldier Campion

(FOR ISHBEL AGED FIVE)

Campion so small and brave
Shaking in the Cornish wind
Guard the lady well whose arms
Are bright upon your shield.

When below your hill you see
The banners of an army come
Cry out with your little voice
And growl upon your little drum.

The ragged robin at your side
Shall your gallant sergeant be
And the elver in the pool
Your admiral upon the sea.

Campion red, upon your hill
Shaking in the Cornish gale,
Guard the lady for whose sake
I have written down this tale.

The Broad Close

Come dodge the deathblow if you can
   Between a word or two.
Forget the times we've fallen out
   Or who we've fallen through.
For you are me all over again
   Except where you are new.

I may have hurled my skills away,
   Such as they are, but me,
Well, I'm jackeasy if I slip
   The muse a length for she
Appreciates the starkest man
   Her length and breadth to be.

But there you are. Grandfather whirrs
   And strikes dead on his time.
He was the rude oak of his day
   For the bluenose and the sperm
Till the midnight sun with a flensing spear
   Yelled and struck him dumb.

And there you were by Clydeside clad,
   Heir to a difficult home.
But here we fall as men alive
   Within this very room.
Read me your aid as the word falls
   Or all falls to bedlam.

'Twas on (or shall be on) a black
   Bitter Saturday night.
I sat broke in a black drouth

And not a dram in sight.
I heard a homeward nightfaller
   Passing his courage out.

I think he was an old man
   By that dribbling pace.
And then he must have followed it
   And fell in the Broad Close,
And as he fell he jingled and
   I never heard him rise.

But that's all by the way. It was
   (As Meg was the first to find)
On such a night as would unman
   (It monkeyed with the gland.)
The best of us or even to freeze
   Them off a brass band.

I fell awake. My forty winks
   Fled as before a ghost.
I rose and looked out and the cobbles
   Looked in with a staring frost.
(Hang your coat on the first word.
   You lift it from the last.)

They were my dead burning to catch
   Me up in a time to be.
To think they were once my joke and grief
   As real as this bad knee.
But now they are to the grave gone
   That's digged in memory.

The glass has blinded with a breath.
   All that sight is out.

Why should they stare from the grave again
   At me they died to meet?
The sweet oil walks within the wick
   And gulls on the shore bleat.

Away with them all! Now can you sing
   The Smashing of the Van?
You'll not be in your better form
   But I'm an easy man.
Just strike up one with a go and I'll
   Beat out the time till dawn.

O sing my grief as joke through
   All the sad counterparts.
Your voice is mine all over again,
   The voice of a lad of parts,
The voice out of the whisky bush,
   The reek in the breathless arts.

But stop. Allow me time to tell.
   The tongue on the quay told.
And told me it was time my great
   Inheritance was hauled.
(O never have heed of dead folk
   If you find them afield.)

I took my weapons up and went
   With hardly a word to spare.
And I wore my father's error for
   That I'll always wear.
But there was no bad in me
   As I went from that door.

And may he strike me down without
   The turn of a holy hair.
If there was any bad in me
   When I went from that door.
And as I went my breath aghast
   Proceeded me before.

I tell it here upon the old
   Voices and the new,
And let them have their fling between
   Meanings out of the true
That they may make a harmony
   That's proper to us two.

And I went out on any word
   Would bring me to myself
And they were cold and hard words
   And cut my truth in half.
But I was blind till the frost blazed
   Me suddenly wakerife.

I heard the blindman's hedge and all
   The white roar of the sea.
I saw the deaf man's bell that struck
   The ice from off the tree.
And then I heard but a thin sound,
   Went straight to where he lay.

And O it is not to ask me by
   The flensing or the spear,
Or the grey table of the grave
   That writes between us here.
But it is enough to ask me by
   His likeness I wear.

'Come dodge the death blow, old man
    For I see you are not fain
To yield me my inheritance,
    But you will feel no pain.
You died to meet me once and now
    You are to die again.

And cock your ears and leave no word
    Unturned that I am in.
For the gale will skelp upon the firth
    And drive the hailing stone,
And you out of the weather where
    There is not flesh or bone.

If I am you all over again
    By the joke and by the grief
Dodge if you can this very word,
    For it is the flensing knife.'
And I have put it in his breast
    And taken away his life.

I turned it round for all that
    Seeing he did not stir.
And the Broad Close was bitter and
    Is bitter at this hour.
The sweet oil walks within the wick
    And gulls bleat on the shore.

Both wit and weapons must the king
    Have over all alive
And over all his dead that they
    Do him only love.
And wit and weapons must the king
Have down into the grave.

To My Mother

Under (not ground but the mind's)
Thunder you rest on memory's
Daily aloneness as rest
My steps to a great past.

My memory saves its breath.
Its flowing stronghold with
Crowds of the day and night
Changes them each heartbeat.

In words I change them further
Away from the parent fire.
Look. Into life or out?
What son did you inherit?

The flowing strongheld Clyde
Rests me my earliest word
That has ever matchlessly
Changed me towards the sea.

That deep investment speaks
Over ship-cradles and derricks
And ebbs to a perfection's
Deadly still anatomies.

Sometimes like loneliness
Memory's crowds increase.
Suddenly some man I am
So finds himself endless stream

Of stepping away from his
Last home, I crave an ease
Stopped for a second dead
Out of the speaking flood.

Under (not ground but the words)
You rest with speaking hordes.

Listen Put on Morning

Listen. Put on morning.
Waken into falling light.
A man's imagining
Suddenly may inherit
The handclapping centuries
Of his one minute on earth.
And hear the virgin juries
Talk with his own breath
To the corner boys of his street.
And hear the Black Maria
Searching the town at night.
And hear the playropes caa
The sister Mary in.
And hear Willie and Davie
Among bracken of Narnain
Sing in a mist heavy
With myrtle and listeners.
And hear the higher town
Weep a petition of fears
At the poorhouse close upon
The public heartbeat.
And hear the children tig
And run with my own feet
Into the netting drag
Of a suiciding principle.
Listen. Put on lightbreak.
Waken into miracle.
The audience lies awake
Under the tenements
Under the sugar docks
Under the printed moments.

The centuries turn their locks
And open under the hill
Their inherited books and doors
All gathered to distil
Like happy berry pickers
One voice to talk to us.
Yes listen. It carries away
The second and the years
Till the heart's in a jacket of snow
And the head's in a helmet white
And the song sleeps to be wakened
By the morning ear bright.
Listen. Put on morning.
Waken into falling light.

The Fifteen Devices

When who we think we are is suddenly
Flying apart, splintered into
Acts we hardly recognize
As once our kin's curious children,
I find myself turning my head
Round to observe and strangely
Accept expected astonishments
Of myself manifest and yet
Bereft somehow as I float
Out in an old-fashioned slow
Motion in all directions. I hope
A value is there lurking somewhere.

Whether it is the words we try
To hold on to or some other
Suggestion of outsideness at least
Not ourselves, it is a naked
State extremely uncomfortable.

My fifteen devices of shadow and brightness
Are settling in and the Madron
Morning accepts them in their place.
Early early the real as any
Badger in the black wood
Of Madron is somewhere going
His last round, a creature of words
Waiting to be asked to help me
In my impure, too-human purpose.

With me take you. Where shall you find us?
Somewhere here between the prised

Open spaces in the flying
Apart words. For then it was
All the blown, black wobblers
Came over on the first wind
To let me see themselves looking
In from a better high flocking
Organization than mine. They make
Between them a flag flying standing
For their own country. Down the Fore
Street run the young to the school bell.

Shall I pull myself together into
Another place? I can't follow
The little young clusters of thoughts
Running down the summer side.

My fifteen devices in my work
Shop of shadow and brightness have
Their places as they stand ready
To go out to say Hello.

Johann Joachim Quantz's First Lesson

So that each person may quickly find that
Which particularly concerns him, certain metaphors
Convenient to us within the compass of this
Lesson are to be allowed. It is best I sit
Here where I am to speak on the other side
Of language. You, of course, in your own time
And incident (I speak in the small hours.)
Will listen from your side. I am very pleased
We have sought us out. No doubt you have read
My Flute Book. Come. The Guild clock's iron men
Are striking out their few deserted hours
And here from my high window Brueghel's winter
Locks the canal below. I blow my fingers.

Here Next the Chair I was when Winter Went

Here next the chair I was when winter went
Down looking for distant bothies of love
And met birch-bright and by the blows of March
The farm bolder under and the din of burning.

I was what the whinfire works on towns
An orator from hill to kitchen dances.
In booths below bridges that spanned the crowds
Tinkers tricked glasses on lips and saw my eyes.

Like making a hut of fingers cupped for tears
Love burned my bush that was my burning mother.
The hoodiecrow in smoke in a wobbling wind
If a look is told for fortune saw my death.

So still going out in the morning of ash and air
My shovel swings. My tongue is a sick device.
Fear evening my boot says. The chair sees iceward
In the bitter hour so visible to death.

Master Cat and Master Me

(FOR ANTÓINE ÓMÁILLE)

The way I see it is that Master
Me is falling out with Servant
Me and understairs is live
With small complaints and clattering.

The dust is being too quickly
Feathered off my dear objects.
On the other hand I find myself
Impeded where I want to go.

Even the cat (He has no name.)
Is felinely aware that Master
House's bosom is not what
It used to be. The kitchen door

Swings on its hinges singing on
A foreign pitch. The mice have new
Accents and their little scurries
Have acquired a different grace.

At this time the light is always
Anxious to be away. The mantel
Brasses flicker and Malcolm Mooney's
Walrus tusk gleams yellow.

Who let you in? Who pressed
The cracked Master's cup on you?
I will show you out through
The Master's door to the Servant world.

Don't let Master Cat out.
He has to stay and serve with me.
His Master now must enter
The service of the Master Sea.

Five Visitors to Madron

I

In the small hours on the other side
Of language with my chair drawn
Up to the frightening abstract
Table of silence, taps. A face
Of white feathers turns my head
To suddenly see between the mad
Night astragals her looking in
Or wanted this to happen. She
Monster muse old bag or. Something
Dreamed is yes you're welcome always
Desired to drop in. It was your bleached
Finger on the pane which startled me
Although I half-expected you
But not you as you are but whoever
Would have looked in instead, another
More to my liking, not so true.

He realized it was a mistake. Closing
The door of the tomb afterwards
Secretly he thanked whoever
He could imagine to thank, some quick
Thought up thankable god of the moment.

II

As slow as distant spray falling
On the nether rocks of a headland never
Encountered but through the eye, the first
Of morning's ghost in blue palely
Hoisted my reluctant lid.
Watch what you say I said and watched

The day I uttered taking shape
To hide me in its bright bosom.

Like struck flints black flocking jack
Daws wheel over the Madron roofs.

III

I am longing not really longing
For what dont tell me let me think.
Or else I have to settle for
That step is that a step outside
At my back a new eddy of air?

And left these words at a loss to know
What form stood watching behind me
Reading us over my shoulder. I said
Now that you have come to stand
There rank-breathed at my elbow I will
Not be put off. This message must
Reach the others without your help.

IV

And met the growing gaze willing
To give its time to me to let
Itself exchange discernments
If that surely it said is what
I wanted. Quick panics put out
A field of images round me to
Look back out at it from and not
Be gazed out of all composure.
And found my research ridiculously
Ending forced to wear a mask
Of a held-up colander to peer

Through as the even gaze began
Slowly to abate never having asked
Me if I had recognized an old
Aspect of need there once my own.

Terror-spots itch on my face now.
My mind is busy hanging up
Back in their places imagination's
Clever utensils. I scratch my cheek.

V

When the fifth came I had barely drawn
A breath in to identify who
I newly am in my new old house
In Madron near the slaughterhouse.

The hint was as though a child running
Late for school cried and seemed
To have called my name in the morning
Hurrying and my name's wisp
Elongated. Leaves me here
Nameless at least very without
That name mine ever to be called
In that way different again.

Clusters Travelling Out

I

Clearly I tap to you clearly
Along the plumbing of the world
I do not know enough, not
Knowing where it ends. I tap
And tap to interrupt silence into
Manmade durations making for this
Moment a dialect for our purpose.
TAPTAP. Are you reading that taptap
I send out to you along
My element? O watch. Here they come
Opening and shutting Communication's
Gates as they approach, History's
Princes with canisters of gas
Crystals to tip and snuff me out
Strangled and knotted with my kind
Under the terrible benevolent roof.

Clearly they try to frighten me
To almost death. I am presuming
You know who I am. To answer please
Taptap quickly along the nearest
Metal. When you hear from me
Again I will not know you. Whoever
Speaks to you will not be me.
I wonder what I will say.

II

Remember I am here O not else
Where in this quick disguise, this very
Thought that's yours for a moment. I sit
Here behind this tempered mesh.

I think I hear you hearing me.
I think I see you seeing me.
I suppose I am really only about
Two feet away. You must excuse
Me, have I spoken to you before?
I seem to know your face from some
One else I was, that particular
Shadow head on the other side
Of the wire in the VISITORS ROOM.

I am learning to speak here in a way
Which may be useful afterwards.
Slops in hand we shuffle together,
Something to look forward to
Behind the spy-hole. Here in our concrete
Soundbox we slide the jargon across
The watching air, a lipless language
Necessarily squashed from the side
To make its point against the rules.
It is our poetry such as it is.

Are you receiving those clusters
I send out travelling? Alas
I have no way of knowing or
If I am overheard here.
Is that (It is.) not what I want?

The slaughterhouse is next door.
Destroy this. They are very strict.

III

Can you see my As and Ys semaphore
Against the afterglow on the slaughterhouse
Roof where I stand on the black ridge
Waving my flagging arms to speak?

IV

Corridors have their character. I know well
The ring of government boots on our concrete.
Malcolm's gone now. There's nobody to shout to.
But when they're not about in the morning I shout
HOY HOY HOY and the whole corridor rings
And I listen while my last HOY turns the elbow
With a fading surprised difference of tone and loses
Heart and in dwindling echoes vanishes away.
Each person who comes, their purpose precedes them
In how they walk. You learn to read that.
Sometimes the step's accompanied by metal
Jingling and metrical, filled with invention.
Metal opened and slammed is frightening. I try
To not be the first to speak. There is nothing to say.
Burn this. I do not dislike this place. I like
Being here. They are very kind. It's doing me good.

V

If this place I write from is real then
I must be allegorical. Or maybe
The place and myself are both the one
Side of the allegory and the other
Side is apart and still escaped
Outside. And where do you come in
With your musical key-ring and brilliant
Whistle pitched for the whipped dog?

And stands loving to recover me,
Lobe-skewers clipped to his swelling breast,
His humane-killer draped with a badged
Towel white as snow. And listen,
Ventriloquized for love his words
Gainsay any deep anguish left
For the human animal. O dear night
Cover up my beastly head.

VI

Take note of who stands at my elbow listening
To all I say but not to all you hear.
She comes on Wednesdays, just on Wednesdays,
And today I make a Wednesday. On and off
I decide to make her my half-cousin Brigit
Back from the wrack and shingle of the Long Loch.
You yourself need pretend nothing. She
Is only here as an agent. She could not
On her own carry a message to you either
Written or dreamed by word of her perfect mouth.

Look. Because my words are stern and frown
She is somewhere wounded. She goes away. You see
It hasn't been a good Wednesday for her. For you
Has it been a good Wednesday? Or is yours Tuesday?

VII

When the birds blow like burnt paper
Over the poorhouse roof and the slaughter
House and all the houses of Madron,
I would like to be out of myself and
About the extra, ordinary world
No matter what disguise it wears
For my sake, in my love.

It would be better than beside the Dneiper,
The Bramahputra or a green daughter
Tributary of the Amazon.

But first I must empty my shit-bucket
And hope my case (if it can be found)
Will come up soon. I thought I heard
My name whispered on the vine.

Surrounded by howls the double-shifting
Slaughterhouse walls me in. High
On the wall I have my blue square
Through which I see the London–Cairo
Route floating like distant feathers.

I hear their freezing whistles. Reply
Carefully. They are cracking down.
Dont hurry away. I am waiting for
A message to come in now.

KATHLEEN RAINE

FROM STONE AND FLOWER (1943)

The Silver Stag

My silver stag is fallen – on the grass
Under the birch-leaves he lies, my king of the woods,
That I followed on the mountain, over the swift streams.
He is gone under the leaves, under the past.

On the horizon of the dawn, he stood,
The target of my eager sight; that shone
Oh from the sun, or from my kindled heart –
Outlined in sky, shaped on the infinite.

What, so desiring, was my will with him,
What wished-for union of blood or thought
In single passion held us, hunter and victim?
Already gone, when into the branched woods I pursued
  him.

Mine he is now, my desired, my awaited, my beloved,
Quiet he lies, as I touch the contours of his proud head,
Mine, this horror, this carrion of the wood,
Already melting underground, into the air, out of the
  world.

Oh, the stillness, the peace about me
As the garden lives on, the flower bloom,
The fine grass shimmers, the flies burn,
And the stream, the silver stream, runs by.

Lying for the last time down on the green ground
In farewell gesture of self-love, softly he curved

To rest the delicate foot that is in my hand,
Empty as a moth's discarded chrysalis.

My bright yet blind desire, your end was this
Death, and my winged heart murderous
Is the world's broken heart, buried in his,
Between whose antlers starts the crucifix.

The Crystal Skull

At the focus of thought there is no face,
the focus of the sun is in crystal with no shadow.
Death of the victim is the power of the god.

Out of the eyes is the focus of love,
the face of love is the sun, that all see,
the skull of the victim is the temple of sight.

The eyes of the victim are the crystal of divination.
Sun clears the colours of life.
The crystal of the skull is the work of the sun.

The stone of my destruction casts no shadow.
The sun kills perfectly with the stroke of noon.
The clarity of the crystal is the atonement of the god.

The perfection of man is the pride of death,
the crystal skull is the perpetuity of life.
The power of the god is the taking of love.

The perfection of light is the destruction of the world,
death and love turn the faces of day and night.
The illumination of the skull is the joy of the god.

On Leaving Ullswater

I

The air is full of a farewell –
deserted by the silver lake
lies the wild world, overturned.
Cities rise where mountains fell,
the furnace where the phoenix burned.

II

The lake is in my dream,
the tree is in my blood,
the past is in my bones,
the flowers of the wood
I love with long past loves.
I fear with many deaths
the presence of the night,
and in my memory read
the scripture of the leaves –
        Only myself how strange
        to the strange present come!

The Wind of Time

Time blows a tempest – how the days run high,
Deep graves are open between hour and hour,
A current sweeps the streets and houses by
Too fast to board them. Cities are wrecked by night
And we left drowning in this empty dawn,
No land is seaworthy, no bird in sight.

And on the shores, after the tempest lie
Fragments of past delight, and of past selves,
Dead rooms and houses with the strangled shells.

FROM LIVING IN TIME (1946)

The Still Pool

The still pool! Give here grace
Even of reflected trees, reflected stars, though these
That rest upon the water's quiet surface
Are not tangible leaves, are not uplifted skies.

Yet not unreal. Like painting and symphony
They draw their veil
Of true illusion, rainbow over the grey.

Quiet semblances. Real otherwise but not less than these
Sombre deep pools, where, like troubled thoughts
Inhabits the unsmiling water-life.

(Native to that state only – as to selves
Pains, lusts, pleasures, and desires – these die
Translated to the green earth and the open sky.)

Not to that under-world are the sky's stars native, nor its
    birds,
Nor the abundant trees, whose roots
Stir in the water's depths an impulse to ascend

Into those leaves and boughs, into those flowers
Out of an element whose nature is to fall
Yet, against nature, may in nature rise.

The pool holds their images: to weed and fish not real
They rest upon the surface, colour and form of things
True, though not here as they to themselves elsewhere
    are.

FROM THE PYTHONESS (1949)

Air

Element that utters doves, angels and cleft flames,
The bees of Helicon and the cloudy houses,
Impulse of music and the word's equipoise,

Dancer that never wearies of the dance
That prints in the blown dust eternal wisdom
Or carves its abstract sculptures in the snow,
The wind unhindered passes beyond its trace.

But from a high fell on a summer day
Sometimes below you may see the air like water,
The dazzle of the light upon its waves
That flow unbroken to the end of the world.

The bird of god descends between two moments
Like silence into music, opening a way through time.

Word Made Flesh

Word whose breath is the world-circling atmosphere,
Word that utters the world that turns the wind,
Word that articulates the bird that speeds upon the air,

Word that blazes out the trumpet of the sun,
Whose silence is the violin-music of the stars,
Whose melody is the dawn, and harmony the night,

Word traced in water of lakes, and light on water,
Light on still water, moving water, waterfall
And water colours of cloud, of dew, of spectral rain,

Word inscribed on stone, mountain range upon range of
    stone,
Word that is fire of the sun and fire within
Order of atoms, crystalline symmetry,

Grammar of five-fold rose and six-fold lily,
Spiral of leaves on a bough, helix of shells,
Rotation of twining plants on axes of darkness and light,

Instinctive wisdom of fish and lion and ram,
Rhythm of generation in flagellate and fern,
Flash of fin, beat of wing, heartbeat, beat of the dance,

Hieroglyph in whose exact precision is defined
Feather and insect-wing, refraction of multiple eyes,
Eyes of the creatures, oh myriadfold vision of the world,

Statement of mystery, how shall we name
A spirit clothed in world, a world made man?

Isis Wanderer

This too is an experience of the soul
The dismembered world that once was the whole god
Whose broken fragments now lie dead.
This passing of reality itself is real.

Gathering under my black cloak the remnants of life
That lie dishonoured among people and places
I search the twofold desert of my solitude,
The outward perished world, and the barren mind.

Once he was present, numinous, in the house of the
   world,
Wearing day like a garment, his beauty manifest
In corn and man as he journeyed down the fertile river.
With love he filled my distances of night.

I trace the contour of his hand fading upon a cloud,
And this his blood flows from a dying soldier's wound.
In broken fields his body is scattered and his limbs lie
Spreadeagled like wrecked fuselage in the sand.

His skull is a dead cathedral, and his crown's rays
Glitter from worthless tins and broken glass.
His blue eyes are reflected from pools in the gutter,
And his strength is the desolate stone of fallen cities.

Oh in the kitchen-midden of my dreams
Turning over the potsherds of past days
Shall I uncover his loved desecrated face?
Are the unfathomed depths of sleep his grave?

Beyond the looming dangerous end of night
Beneath the vaults of fear do his bones lie,
And does the maze of nightmare lead to the power
    within?
Do menacing nether waters cover the fish king?

I piece the divine fragments into the mandala
Whose centre is the lost creative power,
The sun, the heart of God, the lotus, the electron
That pulses world upon world, ray upon ray
That he who lived on the first may rise on the last day.

The World

It burns in the void.
Nothing upholds it.
Still it travels.

Travelling the void
Upheld by burning
Nothing is still.

Burning it travels.
The void upholds it.
Still it is nothing.

Nothing it travels
A burning void
Upheld by stillness.

FROM THE YEAR ONE (1952)

Spell of Creation

Within the flower there lies a seed,
Within the seed there springs a tree,
Within the tree there spreads a wood.

In the wood there burns a fire,
And in the fire there melts a stone,
Within the stone a ring of iron.

Within the ring there lies an O
Within the O there looks an eye,
In the eye there swims a sea,

And in the sea reflected sky,
And in the sky there shines the sun,
Within the sun a bird of gold.

Within the bird there beats a heart,
And from the heart there flows a song,
And in the song there sings a word.

In the word there speaks a world,
A word of joy, a world of grief,
From joy and grief there springs my love.

Oh love, my love, there springs a world,
And on the world there shines a sun
And in the sun there burns a fire,
Within the fire consumes my heart
And in my heart there beats a bird,
And in the bird there wakes an eye,

Within the eye, earth, sea and sky,
Earth, sky and sea within an O
Lie like the seed within the flower.

FROM THREE POEMS OF ILLUSION (1951)

The Mirage

No, I have seen the mirage tremble, seen how thin
The veil stretched over apparent time and space
To make the habitable earth, the enclosed garden.

I saw on a bare hillside an ash-tree stand
And all its intricate branches suddenly
Failed, as I gazed, to be a tree,
And road and hillside failed to make a world.
Hill, tree, sky, distance, only seemed to be
And I saw nothing I could give a name,
Not any name known to the heart.

What failed? The retina received
The differing waves of light, or rays of darkness,
Eyes, hands, all senses brought me
Messages that lifelong I had believed.
Appearances that once composed reality
Here turned to dust, to mist, to motes in the eye
Or like the reflection broken on a pool
The unrelated visual fragments foundered
On a commotion of those deeps
Where earth floats safe, when waves are still.

The living instrument
When fingers gently touch the strings,
Or when a quiet wind
Blows through the reed, makes music of birds,
Song, words, the human voice.
Too strong a blast from outer space,
A blow too heavy breaks and silences

The singer and the song;
A grief too violent
Wrecks the image of the world, on waves whose
    amplitude
Beats beyond the compass of the heart.

The waves subside, the image reassembles:
There was a tree once more, hills, and the world,
But I have seen the emptiness of air
Ready to swallow up the bird in its flight,
Or note of music, or winged word, the void
That traps the rabbit on cropped turf as in a snare,
Lies at the heart of the wren's warm living eggs,
In pollen dust of summer flowers, opens
Within the smallest seed of grass, the abyss
That now and always underlies the hills.

Invocation

Child in the little boat
Come to the land
Child of the seals
Calf of the whale
Spawn of the octopus
Fledgling of cormorant
Gannet and herring-gull,
Come from the sea,
Child of the sun,
Son of the sky.

Safely pass
The mouths of the water,
The mouths of night,
The teeth of the rocks,
The mouths of the wind,
Safely float
On the dangerous waves
Of an ocean sounding
Deeper than red
Darker than violet,
Safely cross
The ground-swell of pain
Of the waves that break
On the shores of the world.

Life everlasting
Love has prepared
The paths of your coming.
Plankton and nekton
Free-swimming pelagic

Spawn of the waters
Has brought you to birth
In the life-giving pools,
Spring has led you
Over the meadows
In fox's fur
Has nestled and warmed you,
With the houseless hare
In the rushes has sheltered
Warm under feathers
Of brooding wings
Safe has hidden
In the grass secretly
Clothed in disguise
Of beetle and grasshopper
Small has laid you
Under a stone.
In the nest of the ants
Myriadfold scattered
In pollen of pine forests
Set you afloat
Like dust on the air
And winged in multitudes
Hatched by the sun
From the mud of rivers.

Newborn you have lain
In the arms of mothers,
You have drawn life
From a myriad breasts,
The mating of animals
Has not appalled you,
The longing of lovers

You have not betrayed,
You have come unscathed
From the field of battle
From famine and plague
You have lived undefiled
In the gutters of cities
We have seen you dancing
Barefoot in villages
You have been to school.
But kept your wisdom.

Child in the little boat,
Come to the land,
Child of the seals.

Seventh Day

Passive I lie, looking up through leaves,
An eye only, one of the eyes of earth
That open at a myriad points at the living surface.
Eyes that earth opens see and delight
Because of the leaves, because of the unfolding of the
    leaves,
The folding, veining, imbrication, fluttering, resting,
The green and deepening manifold of the leaves.

Eyes of the earth know only delight
Untroubled by anything that I am, and I am nothing:
All that nature is, receive and recognize,
Pleased with the sky, the falling water and the flowers,
With bird and fish and the striations of stone.
Every natural form, living and moving
Delights these eyes that are no longer mine
That open upon earth and sky pure vision.
Nature sees, sees itself, is both seer and seen.

This is the divine repose, that watches
The ever-changing light and shadow, rock and sky and
    ocean.

Shells

Reaching down arm-deep into bright water
I gathered on white sand under waves
Shells, drifted up on beaches where I alone
Inhabit a finite world of years and days.
I reached my arm down a myriad years
To gather treasure from the yester-millennial sea-floor,
Held in my fingers forms shaped on the day of creation.

Building their beauty in the three dimensions
Over which the world recedes away from us,
And in the fourth, that takes away ourselves
From moment to moment and from year to year
From first to last they remain in their continuous present.
The helix revolves like a timeless thought,
Instantaneous from apex to rim
Like a dance whose figure is limpet or murex, cowrie or
    golden winkle.

They sleep on the ocean floor like humming-tops
Whose music is the mother-of-pearl octave of the rainbow,
Harmonious shells that whisper for ever in our ears,
'The world that you inhabit has not yet been created.'

Rock

There is stone in me that knows stone,
Substance of rock that remembers the unending
   unending
Simplicity of rest
While scorching suns and ice ages
Pass over rock-face swiftly as days.
In the longest time of all come the rock's changes,
Slowest of all rhythms, the pulsations
That raise from the planet's core the mountain ranges
And weather them down to sand on the sea-floor.

Remains in me record of rock's duration.
My ephemeral substance was still in the veins of the
   earth from the beginning,
Patient for its release, not questioning
When, when will come the flowering, the flowing,
The pulsing, the awakening, the taking wing,
The long longed-for night of the bridegroom's coming.

There is stone in me that knows stone,
Whose sole state is stasis
While the slow cycle of the stars whirls a world of rock
Through light-years where in nightmare I fall crying
'Must I travel fathomless distance for ever and ever?'
All that is in me of the rock, replies
'For ever, if it must be: be, and be still; endure.'

The Moment

Never, never again
This moment, never
These slow ripples
Across smooth water,
Never again these
Clouds white and grey
In sky sharp crystalline
Blue as the tern's cry
Shrill in light air
Salt from the ocean,
Sweet from flowers.

Here coincide
The long histories
Of forms recurrent
That meet at a point
And part in a moment,
The rapid waves
Of wind and water
And slower rhythm
Of rock weathering
And land sinking.

In teeming pools
The life cycle
Of brown weed
Is intersecting
The frequencies
Of diverse shells
Each with its variant
Arc or spiral

Spun from a point
In tone and semitone
Of formal octave.

Here come soaring
White gulls
Leisurely wheeling
In air over islands
Sea pinks and salt grass,
Gannet and eider,
Curlew and cormorant
Each a differing
Pattern of ecstasy
Recurring at nodes
In an on-flowing current,
The perpetual species,
Repeated, renewed
By the will of joy
In eggs lodged safe
On perilous ledges.

The sun that rises
Upon one earth
Sets on another,
Swiftly the flowers
Are waxing and waning,
The tall yellow iris
Unfolds its corolla
As primroses wither,
Scrolls of fern
Unroll and midges
Dance for an hour
In the evening air,

The brown moth
From its pupa emerges
And the lark's bones
Fall apart in the grass.

The sun that rose
From the sea this morning
Will never return,
For the broadcast light
That brightens the leaves
And glances on water
Will travel tonight
On its long journey
Out of the universe,
Never this sun,
This world, and never
Again this watcher.

FROM THE HOLLOW HILL (1965)

Golden Flowers

I have travelled so fast that I have come to the waterfall
    of Sgriol:
Curtain of mist, of netted leaves, inviolate leafy vale,
Fragrant veil of green-gold birch and song of the
    green-gold linnet
A shadow withdrawn I enter for ever the sun-filled
    gloaming of Sgriol.

Light you have travelled so far out of the boundless void
From beyond the Isle of Skye over the sound of Sleat
You have laid a path of wonder over the bright sea
And touched with your finger the golden summit of
    Sgriol.

Water you have gathered in mist high over ben Sgriol,
So fast your drifting curtain of rain has fallen
That the noise of the sun-brown burn is filling the glen of
    Sgriol.

Seed you have grown so fast from the mould of the dead
You have unfolded a hundred flowers with golden petals,
The hundred-petalled golden flowers are filled with light
And leaves are moist with the life-giving waters of the
    burn of Sgriol.

Oh sun and water and green-gold flowers, I was here and
    now in the glen of Sgriol.

Light how fast you have travelled on into the abyss

And into ocean the burn that played in the sunlit fern of
    Sgriol.
Seed of miraculous flowers lies cold in the bog,
Sun sets in the beautiful land of the dead beyond the Isle
    of Skye.

The Hollow Hill

(DUN AENGUS AT BRUGH NA BOYNE)
FOR WILLA MUIR IN MEMORY OF EDWIN MUIR

I

Outside, sun, frost, wind, rain,
Lichen, grass-root, bird-claw, scoring thorn
Wear away the stone that seals the tomb,
Erode the labyrinth inscribed in the stone,
Emblem of world and its unwinding
And inwinding volutions of the brain.
On the door out of the world the dead have left this sign.

The moving now has drawn its thread
Tracing the ravelled record of the dead
Through all the wanderings of the living.
Reaching at last the sum of our becoming,
The line inwound into a point again,
The spaces of the world full circle turn
Into the nought where all began.

We cannot look from the world into their house,
Or they look from their house into our sky;
For the low door where we crawl from world to world
Into the earth-cave bends and turns away
To close the hidden state of the dead from the light of day.
The grave is empty, they are gone:
In the last place they were, their clay
Clings crumbling to the roots of trees,
Whose fibres thread their way from earth to earth again.

Crouched in birth-posture in the cave
The ancestors are laid with the unborn,
(For who knows whether to die be not to live)
One worn hand touching the worn stone,
Calling the earth to witness, the other palm
Open to receive whatever falls:
Archaic icon of man's condition.

Yet so the great slabs have leaned three thousand years
That a single beam, shaft, arrow, ray
This dark house of the dead can pierce.
From world to world there is a needle's eye:
Light spans the heavens to find the punctum out,
To touch with finger of life a dead man's heart.

2

It is time, heart, to recall,
To recollect, regather all:
The grain is grown,
Reap what was sown
And bring into the barn your corn.

Those fields of childhood, tall
Meadow-grass and flowers small,
The elm whose dusky leaves
Patterned the sky with dreams innumerable
And labyrinthine vein and vine
And wandering tendrils green,
Have grown a seed so small
A single thought contains them all.

The white birds on their tireless wings return,
Spent feather, flesh and bone let fall,

And the blue distances of sea and sky
Close within the closing eye
As everywhere comes nowhere home.
Draw in my heart
Those golden rays whose threads of light
The visible veil of world have woven,
And through the needle's eye
Upon that river bright
Travels the laden sun
Back from its voyage through the night.

We depart and part,
We fail and fall
Till love calls home
All who our separate lonely ways have gone.

3

The rock is written with the sign
In geometric diamond prison,
Prism, cube and rhomboid, mineral grain,
The frozen world of rigid form
Inexorable in line and plane
At every point where meet and part
The cross-ways of the enduring world.

In curving vault and delicate cone
Each formula of shell and bone
In willow-spray and branching vein,
In teleost's feathered skeleton,
In nerve of bird and human brain
Along its moving axis drawn
Each star of life has gone its way
Tracing the cross-ways of the world.

Here on death's door the hand of man
Has scored our history in the stone,
The emblematic branching tree
That crucifies to line and plane,
Writhes into life in nerve and vein,
Bleeds and runs and cowers and flies,
Resolved into a thought again
From nowhere come to nowhere gone
Those times and distances that span
The enduring cross-ways of the world.

4

The tree of night is spangled with a thousand stars;
Plenum of inner spaces numberless
Of lives secret as leaves on night-elm,
Living maze of wisdom smaragdine
Opens in cell, in membrane, in chain in vein
Infinite number moving in waves that weave
In virgin vagina world-long forest of form,
Cold wild immaculate
Sanctuary of labyrinthine dream.
Lives throng the pleroma
Opening eyes and ears to listen:
Soft, soft they murmur mystery together.

O shadow-tree pinnate in a thousand leaf-ways,
Blades veined fine as insect-scales,
Glittering dust on soul's blue wing,
Full of eyes innumerable and senses fine
As feather green and the green linnet's song,
Arrow-swift wand in flight,
Pollen-grain on the wind
And bitter berry red,

Before you were, you are gone.

Gather a leaf blacker than night and bind it
Over the eye of the sun and the eye of the moon,
Closer than lid of blood, or lid of lead.
There is a banishing ritual for the world,
The great tree and its maze will shrivel
Smaller than pollen-grain, smaller than seed
Of bitter berry red: thought has no size at all;
And some in sorrow's well have seen
In daylight far stars glimmer pale.

5

Whiteness of moonlight builds a house that is not there
On the bare hill,
Wide open house of night,
A gleaming house for those who are nowhere.

All there is valueless we value here,
Our houses are blacked out,
Things are dense darkness,
Nothing the silver surface of the night.
On black grass the untrodden dew is white,
On white birth black leaves glitter,
Bright rings scale the swift salmon river.

The house of the dead is alight,
The stones heaped over the cairn milk-white
In the mind's eye.
They say the charnel-house is a fairy-rath
But none knows where the dead are gone;
Yet when we turn away from a new grave
There is a lightness and a brightness

From those who have passed through the door that is
    nowhere.
Their death is over and done,
Ours still to come,
Grievous and life-long.
Not to be what we are,
Is it to be less, or more?
Waking, or dream, or dreamless sleep, nirvana
Is to be not this, not this.

A dying seabird standing where the burn runs to the
    shore
Between rank leaves and rough stone,
Its nictitating membrane down
Over eyes that knew a wild cold sky,
Head indrawn
Into neck-plumage and wing pinnae furled,
Disturbed in its dying becomes for the last time a gull,
Opens eyes on the world,
Brandishes harsh bill
And then withdraws again to live its death
And unbecome the gull-mask it was.

The dying are the initiates of mystery.
I have heard tell on lonely western shores
Of a light that travels the way the dead go by
Upon an old door in his byre a MacKinnon saw it play
Where afterwards a dead man lay.
A MacIsaac watched it come over the sea
The way a young girl was rowed home from an isle.
It is a different light from ours, they say,
More beautiful.
They tell too of a darkness

That overwhelms and stifles flesh and blood
As the death-coach goes by.
For the living cannot travel by that invisible way;
But when a soul departs, a white bird flies:
Gull, gannet, tern or swan? Not these,
Another kind of bird
Into the emptiness untrammelled soars.

6

One night in a dream
The poet who had died a year ago
Led me up the ancient stair
Of an ancestral tower of stone.
Towards us out of the dark blew such sweet air
It was the warm breath of the spirit, I knew,
Fragrant with wild thyme that grew
In childhood's fields; he led me on,
Touched a thin partition, and was gone.
Beyond the fallen barrier
Bright over sweet meadows rose the sun.

EILEANN CHANAIDH

TO MARGARET AND JOHN LORNE CAMPBELL
OF CANNA

1. The Ancient Speech

A Gaelic bard they praise who in fourteen adjectives
Named the one indivisible soul of his glen;
For what are the bens and the glens but manifold
    qualities,
Immeasurable complexities of soul?
What are these isles but a song sung by island voices?
The herdsman sings ancestral memories
And the song makes the singer wise,
But only while he sings
Songs that were old when the old themselves were young,
Songs of these hills only, and of no isles but these.
For other hills and isles this language has no words.

The mountains are like manna, for one day given,
To each his own:
Strangers have crossed the sound, but not the sound of
    the dark oarsmen
Or the golden-haired sons of kings,
Strangers whose thought is not formed to the cadence of
    waves,
Rhythm of the sickle, oar and milking-pail,
Whose words make loved things strange and small,
Emptied of all that made them heart-felt or bright.

Our words keep no faith with the soul of the world.

2. *Highland Graveyard*

Today a fine old face has gone under the soil;
For generations past women hereabouts have borne
Her same name and stamp of feature.
Her brief identity was not her own
But theirs who formed and sent her out
To wear the proud bones of her clan, and live its story,
Who now receive back into the ground
Worn features of ancestral mould.

A dry-stone wall bounds off the dislimned clay
Of many an old face forgotten and young face gone
From boundless nature, sea and sky.
A wind-withered escalonia like a song
Of ancient tenderness lives on
Some woman's living fingers set as shelter for the dead,
    to tell
In evergreen unwritten leaves,
In scent of leaves in western rain
That one remembered who is herself forgotten.

Many songs they knew who now are silent.
Into their memories the dead are gone
Who haunt the living in an ancient tongue
Sung by old voices to the young,
Telling of sea and isles, of boat and byre and glen;
And from their music the living are reborn
Into a remembered land,
To call ancestral memories home
And all that ancient grief and love our own.

3. The Island Cross

Memories few and deep-grained
Simple and certain mark this Celtic stone
Cross eroded by wind and rain.
All but effaced the hound, the horseman and the strange
   beast,
Yet clear in their signature the ancient soul
Where these were native as to their hunting-hill.

Against grain of granite
Hardness of crystalline rock-form mineral
Form spiritual is countergrained, against nature traced
Man's memories of Paradise and hope of Heaven.
More complex than Patrick's emblem green trifoliate
Patterning the tree soul's windings interlace
Intricate without end its labyrinth.

Their features wind-worn and rain-wasted the man and
   woman
Stand, their rude mere selves
Exposed to the summers and winters of a thousand years.
The god on the cross is man of the same rude race,
By the same hand made from the enduring stone;
And all the winds and waves have not effaced
The vision by Adam seen, those forms of wisdom
From memory of mankind ineffaceable.

4. *Nameless Islets*

Who dreams these isles,
Image bright in eyes
Of sea-birds circling rocky shores
Where waves beat upon rock, or rock-face smiles
Winter and summer, storm and fair?
In eyes of eider clear under ever-moving ripples the dart
    and tremor of life;
Bent-grass and wind-dried heather is a curlew's thought,
Gull gazes into being white and shell-strewn sands.
Joy harsh and strange traced in the dawn
A faint and far mirage; to souls archaic and cold
Sun-warmed stones and fish-giving sea were mother
    stern,
Stone omphalos, birth-caves dark, lost beyond recall.
Home is an image written in the soul,
To each its own: the new-born home to a memory,
Bird-souls, sea-souls, and with them bring anew
The isles that formed the souls, and souls the isles
Are ever building, shell by painted shell
And stone by glittering stone.
The isles are at rest in vision secret and wild,
And high the cliffs in eagle heart exult,
And warm the brown sea-wrack to the seals,
And lichened rocks gray in the buzzard's eye.

5. Stone on High Crag

Still stone
In heart of hill
Here alone
Hoodie and buzzard
By ways of air
Circling come.
From far shine
On wind-worn pinnacle
Star and moon
And sun, sun,
Wings bright in sun
Turn and return.

Centre of wing-spanned
Wheeling ways
Older than menhir
Lichen-roughened
Granite-grained
Rock-red
Rain-pocketed
Wind-buffeted
Heat-holding
Bird-whitened
Beak-worn
Insect-labyrinthine
Turf-embedded
Night-during
Race-remembered
Stand the known.

6. Shadow

Because I see these mountains they are brought low,
Because I drink these waters they are bitter,
Because I tread these black rocks they are barren,
Because I have found these islands they are lost;
Upon seal and seabird dreaming their innocent world
My shadow has fallen.

The Elementals

Say I was where in dream I seemed to be
(Since seeming is a mode of being)
And by analogy say a curtain, veil or door,
A mist, a shadow, an image or a world was gone,
And other semblances behind appeared.
Perhaps a seeming behind the real those giant presences,
But seemed reality behind a seeming.
For they were fraught with power, beauty and awe:
The images before those meanings pale.

What seemed, then, was the world behind the world,
But just behind, and through the thinnest surface,
Not uncreated light nor deepest darkness,
But those abiding essences the rocks and hills and
    mountains
Are to themselves, and not to human sense.
Persons they appeared, but not personified;
Rather rock hill and crag are aspects worn:
Shape-shifters they are, appear and disappear,
Protean assume their guises and transformations
Each in as many forms as eyes behold.

They received me neither as kindred nor as stranger,
Neither welcome nor unwelcome was I in their world;
But I, an exile from their state and station
Made from the place of meeting and parting where I
    stood, the sign
Signature and emblem of the human
Condition of conflict, anguish, love and pain and death
    and joy,
And they in harmony obeyed the cross

Inscribed in the foundation of their world and mine.
From height to depth, circumference to centre
The primal ray, axis of world's darkness
Through all the planes of being descends into the prison
    of the rocks
Where elements in tumultuous voices wordless utter
    their wild credo.

The Eighth Sphere

This litel spot of erthe, that with the se embraced is
Troilus' light ghost beyond the moon ascending
Leaving within this sphere of space we call infinity
Those elements whose warring makes up life sublunary
Travelled in Scipio's track, who from a distant place,
Clear and brilliant in the celestial heights, looked down,
And saw among the sempiternal stars and constellations
This low and heavy world, this rigid prison,
Small and far from heaven shining with borrowed light.

Troilus on the forever shape-shifting surface,
With the beginning saw the end of his desire,
Fading flower of that immortal tree of stars.
Scipio saw Carthage there, how small a spot
Among those seas and continents, but blotting out all
    galaxies
When to the assault he came which razed from time
Dido's bright palaces.

Dreams enlighten the living, dreamers from the dead
    learn wisdom:
Troilus dead and dreaming Scipio saw world as dream
    within dream.
The empirical doctor of souls, sleeping and waking
Between life and death watched the earth turning
Its cloudy globe of continent and ocean
While every sphere and star utters its own sound for ever.

Why then on earth? all ask who have been here,
Why in the body's narrow prison? They say

We are the appointed guardians of this globe, dreaming
    in its own spaces,
Nor without his command by whom the souls are sent
    must we depart;
We see the approaching body of our fate
And go to live each our appointed death, to die our life.
How could we from those heights look back on the
    undone,
Carthage not conquered or Criseyde unloved?
Earth's story must all be told, nothing left out.

I, like that other Cathie, wept in heaven
Until I was set down on a bare January northern moor,
Turned back from my ascent into the freedom of that sky
I ever since have longed to soar again.
But why this here and now only when I loved I knew,
And lifted up with joy the burden of this sorrow.

Images

Again this morning trembles on the swift stream the
    image of the sun
Dimmed and pulsing shadow insubstantial of the bright
    one
That scatters innumerable as eyes these discs of light
    scaling the water.
From a dream foolish and sorrowful I return to this day's
    morning
And words are said as the thread slips away of a ravelled
    story:
'The new-born have forgotten that great burden of pain
'World has endured before you came.'
A marble Eros sleeps in peace unbroken by the fountain
Out of what toils of ever-suffering love conceived?
Only the gods can bear our memories:
We in their lineaments serene
That look down on us with untroubled gaze
Fathom our own mind and what it is
Cleansed from the blood we shed, the deaths we die.

How many tears have traced those still unfading
    presences
Who on dim walls depict spirit's immortal joy?
They look from beyond time on sorrow upon sorrow of
    ours
And of our broken many our whole truth one angel tells,
Ingathers to its golden abiding form the light we scatter,
And winged with unconsuming fire our shattered image
    reassembles.

My load of memory is almost full;
But here and now I see once more mirrored the semblance
    of the radiant source
Whose image the fleet waters break but cannot bear away.

Old Paintings on Italian Walls

Who could have thought that men and women could feel
With consciousness so delicate such tender secret joy?
With finger-tips of touch as fine as music
They greet one another on viols of painted gold
Attuned to harmonies of world with world.
They sense, with inward look and breath withheld,
The stir of invisible presences
Upon the threshold of the human heart alighting,
Angels winged with air, with transparent light,
Archangels with wings of fire and faces veiled.
Their eyes gleam with wisdom radiant from an invisible
    sun.

Others contemplate the mysteries of sorrow.
Some have carried the stigmata, themselves icons
Depicting a passion no man as man can know,
We being ignorant of what we do.
And painted wounded hands are by the same knowledge
    formed,
Beyond the ragged ache that flesh can bear
And we with blunted mind and senses dulled endure.
Giotto's compassionate eyes, rapt in sympathy of grief
See the soul's wounds that hate has given to love,
And those which love must bear
With the spirit that suffers always and everywhere.

Those painted shapes stilled in perpetual adoration
Behold in visible form invisible essences
That hold their gaze entranced through centuries; and we
In true miraculous icons may see still what they see

Though the sacred lineaments grow faint, the outlines
    crumble
And the golden heavens grow dim
Where the Pantocrator shows in vain wounds once held
    precious.
Paint and stone will not hold them to our world
When those who once cast their bright shadows on these
    walls
Have faded from our ken, we from their knowledge
    fallen.

Triad

To those who speak to the many deaf ears attend.
To those who speak to one,
In poet's song and voice of bird,
Many listen; but the voice that speaks to none
By all is heard:
Sound of the wind, music of the stars, prophetic word.

The Eternal Child

A little child
Enters by a secret door, alone,
Was not, and is,
Carrying his torch aflame.

In pilgrim cloak and hood
Many and many come,
Or is it the one child
Again and again?

What journey do they go,
What quest accomplish, task fulfil?
Whence they cannot say,
Whither we cannot tell,
And yet the way they know.

So many innocents,
Reflections in a torrent thrown:
Can any on these treacherous waters cast,
Unmarred, unbroken,
Image the perfect one?

All things seem possible to the new-born;
But each one story tells, one dream
Leaves on the threshold of unbounded night
Where all return
Spent torch and pilgrim shroud.

Scala Coeli

We do not see them come,
Their great wings furled, their boundless forms infolded
Smaller than poppy-seed or grain of corn
To enter the dimensions of our world,
In time to unfold what in eternity they are,
Each a great sun, but dwindled to a star
By the distances they have travelled.

Higher than cupola their bright ingress;
Presences vaster than the vault of night,
Incorporeal mental spaces infinite
Diminished to a point and to a moment brought
Through the everywhere and nowhere invisible door
By the many ways they know
The thoughts of wisdom pass.
In seed that drifts in air, or on the water's flow
They come to us down ages long as dreams
Or instantaneous as delight.

As from seed, tree flower and fruit
Grow and fade like a dissolving cloud,
Or as the impress of the wind
Makes waves and ripples spread,
They move unseen across our times and spaces.
We try to hold them, trace on walls
Of cave, cave-temple or monastic cell their shadows cast:
Animal-forms, warriors, dancers, winged angels, words
    of power
On precious leaves inscribed in gold or lapis lazuli,
Or arabesques in likeness of the ever-flowing.

They show us gardens of Paradise, holy mountains
Where water of life springs from rock or lion's mouth;
Walk with us unseen, put into our hands emblems,
An ear of corn, pine-cone, lotus, looking-glass or chalice;
As dolphin, peacock, hare or moth or serpent show
    themselves,
Or human-formed, a veiled bride, a boy bearing a torch,
Shrouded or robed or crowned, four-faced,
Sounding lyre or sistrum, or crying in bird-voices;
Water and dust and light
Reflect their images as they slowly come and swiftly pass.

We do not see them go
From visible into invisible like gossamer in the sun.
Bodies by spirit raised
Fall as dust to dust when the wind drops,
Moth-wing and chrysalis.
Those who live us and outlive us do not stay,
But leave empty their semblances, icons, bodies
Of long-enduring gold, or the fleet golden flower
On which the Buddha smiled.
In vain we look for them where others found them,
For by the vanishing stair of time immortals are for ever
    departing;
But while we gaze after the receding vision
Others are already descending through gates of ivory and
    horn.

FROM LAST THINGS

2

All is judged,
The shadow by the leaf,
Flower by star,
The great tree by its seed.
The perfect is not in time
Where all is marred;

But lucid forms
Cast their images
Upon the waters:
Their faces, veiled or radiant, are always
    beautiful,
For we imagine them,
They are the aspects of our wisdom.
They bring us messages, intellections,
Impart a mystery,
Could tell us more, if we could hold their gaze.
They play on delicate instruments of joy,
Or cry in harmony the chord of creation,
Tone and overtone,
And when their trumpets sound
The doom of the world is a great music
Wrecking our images on its waves.
From regions of mind forgotten,
The frontiers of our consciousness invading
The Pantocrator raises no hand of power
When all is judged,
The shadow by the real
Being in recollection what it is,
We what we are.

FROM SOLILOQUIES UPON LOVE

3

They pass unnoticed, the moulded lips of the goddess, the
    athlete's stance,
The grace of the shoe-shine kouroi everyone drives away.
Young Athenians at a café table gesturing with nimble
    wrists
Have those full pencilled eyes, those profiles, lacking
    only the beard of Odysseus,
Painters of amphorae depicted three thousand years ago,
    that beauty of race.
A paper towel handed with archaic gesture of sculptured
    choephorae
Bearing upon open palms an offering to the gods; the
    great hurl of Poseidon
Obscured in cement-dust; a beggar-girl walking like a
    caryatid
Alone in her misery as banished Electra,
Lingers in her exile at the 'bus terminus for Chalchis,
Where Agamemnon's other daughter was sacrificed.
They sell indifferent skills for menial wages, whose
    beauty was once beyond price,
Themselves least of all knowing what in such fleeting
    forms old sculptors saw:
Our age has other values.

The Venus of the Cyclades has no face: the crude act she
    celebrates
Requires none: those simple ancestors prized the mons
    veneris, not the eyes or braided hair.
Yet something stood apart from the act of lust, to depict
    a triangle, a shell,

A megalith at once phallus and man with eyes and
    sword: the essentials.
Such simple aspects are yet human; knowledge begins in
    wonder,
And imagination first gave to the crude genitals divine
    mana
Before love could endure to stand apart and contemplate
    entire
Perfection of embodied soul, man, woman, lion, sea-horse,
    ideas of beauty.
Body's unopened eyes never could see that young
    charioteer
So lightly holding the reins, composed, centred in his
    own solitude, remote;
Nor the wind-flower kore on her tomb who with inverted
    torch is departing
With the psychopompos whose ankle-bones are winged
    for flight from world to world.
Soul journeys from body into its own perfection
As pure the moon rides clear of dissolving shadow of
    shapeless cloud.

Love, blind to imperfection, sees only the perfect;
But from how great a distance the inviolate casts its images
Whose gleams upon our waters ignorance plunges after;
To body a seeming that is not, whose being eludes
    passion's embrace.
No-one has possessed beauty: how can we from an
    intellection dream of requited love?
It is we who are possessed, drawn beyond earth's
    downward pull of flesh and blood
Into another sphere: beauty confers the gift of exile.

5

Your gift to me was a grey stone cast upon a wild shore, traced over
With calligraphy of inscrutable life. A marine annelid
With stroke as free as by master-brush, one fluent word
Has written with its life in the record of the logos,
Yet lacked senses to see its delicate coils and meanders of white masonry.
Mind unknown that blind plasm signed
With weight and drift of sea, of wave-refracted light, and stress of spirit
Omnipresent in every part, universal being here imprinted.
The number-loving Greeks built their white temples
To Apollo of the measured and Aphrodite the veiled source:
Does the same harmony inform those marble shells,
The word that is and means always and everywhere the same?
Your message of life to life was written on the sea-floor before we were;
Serpentine, strange and clear
The deep knowledge we share, who are not the knowers but the known.
You gave and I received as beauty what the logos writes:
Intelligible, though not to us, the inscription on the stone.

MORE ABOUT PENGUINS

Penguinews, which appears every month, contains details of all the new books issued by Penguins as they are published. From time to time it is supplemented by *Penguins in Print*, which is a complete list of all books published by Penguins which are in print. (There are well over three thousand of these.)

A specimen copy of *Penguinews* will be sent to you free on request, and you can become a subscriber for the price of the postage. For a year's issues (including the complete lists) please send 4s. if you live in the United Kingdom, or 8s. if you live elsewhere. Just write to Dept EP, Penguin Books Ltd, Harmondsworth, Middlesex, enclosing a cheque or postal order, and your name will be added to the mailing list.

Some other Poetry books published by Penguins are described on the following pages.

Note: *Penguinews* and *Penguins in Print* are not available in the U.S.A. or Canada

CHILDREN OF ALBION

POETRY OF THE 'UNDERGROUND' IN BRITAIN

Edited by Michael Horovitz

Here at last is the 'secret' generation of British poets whose work could hitherto be discovered only through their own bush telegraph of little magazines and lively readings. These are the energies which have almost completely dispelled the arid critical climate of the 'fifties' and engineered a fresh renaissance of 'the voice of the bard' –

The anthology contains many of the best poems of

Pete Brown	Dave Cuncliffe
Roy Fisher	Lee Harwood
Spike Hawkins	Anselm Hollo
Bernard Kops	Tom McGrath
Adrian Mitchell	Edwin Morgan
Neil Oram	Tom Pickard
Tom Raworth	Chris Torrance
Alex Trocchi	Gael Turnbull

– and *fifty* others – from John Arden to Michael X –

It is edited by Michael Horovitz, with a Blakean cornucopia of 'afterwords' which trace the development of oral and jazz poetry – the Albert Hall Incarnation of 1965 – the influences of the great American and Russian spokesmen – and the diverse lyric, political, visioning and revolutionary orientations of these new poets.

BRITISH POETRY SINCE 1945

Edited with an introduction by Edward Lucie-Smith

British Poetry Since 1945 is the first largely comprehensive anthology of poetry written during this period in England, Scotland, Wales and Northern Ireland. The anthology is arranged to show how the various styles and manners current during the quarter of a century under review relate to one another. Critical notes on as many as 83 poets that are represented, and on their work, as well as bibliographies of each poet's main books make this anthology an ideal introduction to recent British poetry. For those readers already familiar with the field, *British Poetry Since 1945* will prove an invaluable source of reference.

HUGH MACDIARMID SELECTED POEMS

Selected and edited by David Craig and John Manson

This book aims to make more readily available a comprehensive selection from the work of a poet who exacts attention on the same level as the accepted masters of modern poetry. For although MacDiarmid was working at the highest level from the early 20s to the later 30s, most of his work has been available in very limited editions, and some not published at all. In his more complex and fluent philosophical poetry, such as *By Wauchopeside* and *Water of Life,* and in such poems as *The Seamless Garment* and *Lo! A Child is Born,* he is at least the equal of Auden and Yeats. For those readers unfamiliar with literary or spoken Scots, a useful glossary of the most difficult words has been added at the foot of each page.

PENGUIN BOOKS OF VERSE

The Penguin Book of Animal Verse
The Penguin Book of Chinese Verse
The Penguin Book of Contemporary Verse
The Penguin Book of Elizabethan Verse
The Penguin Book of Romantic English Verse
The Penguin Book of English Verse
The Penguin Book of French Verse
(Three Volumes)
The Penguin Book of German Verse
The Penguin Book of Irish Verse
The Penguin Book of Italian Verse
The Penguin Book of Japanese Verse
The Penguin Book of Restoration Verse
The Penguin Book of Russian Verse
The Penguin Book of Satirical Verse
The Penguin Book of Scottish Verse
The Penguin Book of Sick Verse
The Penguin Book of South African Verse
The Penguin Book of Spanish Verse
The Penguin Book of Twentieth-Century German Verse
The Penguin Book of Victorian Verse
The Penguin Book of Welsh Verse

THE PENGUIN MODERN POETS

All the earlier volumes in this series are still available. The
more recent volumes are:

*Not for sale in the U.S.A.
†Not for sale in the U.S.A. or Canada